EAT LIKE YOU GIVE A FUCK

COOKING IS ART

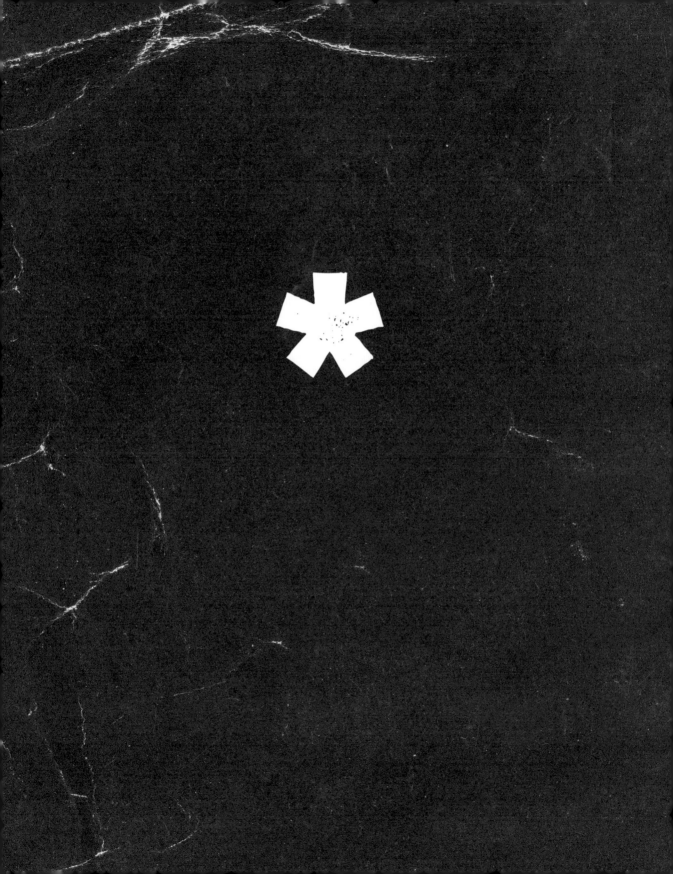

Hungry As Hell

MEALS TO LIVE BY, FLAVOR TO DIE FOR

A **BAD✱MANNERS** COOKBOOK

SPHERE

SPHERE

First published in the USA in 2023 by Rodale Books, an imprint of
Random House, a division of Penguin Random House LLC
First Published in Great Britain 2023 by Sphere

13 5 7 9 10 8 6 4 2

Design by Kara Plikaitis and Nick Hensley
Illustrations by Nick Hensley
Photographs by Matt Holloway
Recipes by Michelle Davis

A CIP catalogue record for this book is available from the British Library.

ISBN 9-780-7515-8136-2

Printed and bound in China by C & C OFFSET PRINTING CO LTD

Papers used by Sphere are from well-managed forests
and other responsible sources.

Sphere
An imprint of
Little, Brown Book Group
Carmelite House
50 Victoria Embankment
London EC4Y 0DZ

An Hachette UK Company
www.hachette.co.uk

www.littlebrown.co.uk

"After a good dinner one can forgive anybody, even one's own relatives."

—Oscar Wilde

Cont

ents

Introduction

Everyone loves to cook, until they don't. This is one of the biggest things we've learned since the release of our first book, *Bad Manners: The Official Cookbook*, almost a decade ago. Everyone wants delicious, life-changing, healthful food, but when it's 7:45 p.m. we'll frantically reach for the chips and make depressing microwave nachos. Our goals, preferences, and plans fall apart under the weight of everyday life. We want jeweled rice and homemade soup but only leave enough time for dino nuggets.

You can't manifest dinner. We've tried.

There's just too much shit to do before you sit down to eat. All the technology we've brought into our lives under the guise of ease have turned into attention and time thieves. We endlessly scroll as we wait for room-temp takeout to appear at our door. We swear this is faster than cooking for ourselves despite all the signs to the contrary. We build communities with brands instead of each other. We save recipes we'll never make time to cook, bookmark workouts we'll never even start. We are starving for real food and real connections.

We're hungry as hell and bet you are, too.

Modern food media isn't making any of this better. Even legacy names are being lost in a quagmire of conspicuous maximalism, wellness snake oil, and functioning as a megaphone for the latest campaign from major food brands. Ten years ago, it wasn't this bad. The plant-based food revolution was gaining momentum in large part due to independent voices entering the food fray thanks to blogs. You know, like us. It felt hopeful. But now what was seen as a fringe way to eat is considered big business. We're tired of reading articles about far-flung restaurants with $700 tasting menus, new lab meats years from viability, and watching videos of beautiful food that's too costly and time-consuming for anyone not chasing clicks to prepare. It's fucking exhausting. We're tired of arguing whether a hot dog is a sandwich, whether you should describe your diet as "plant-based" or "vegan." When all food is branded, who talks about cooking dinner? With the

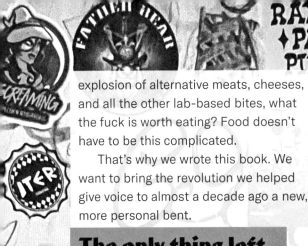

explosion of alternative meats, cheeses, and all the other lab-based bites, what the fuck is worth eating? Food doesn't have to be this complicated.

That's why we wrote this book. We want to bring the revolution we helped give voice to almost a decade ago a new, more personal bent.

The only thing left for us to do here is get your ass in the kitchen.

Not just occasionally, but as the default. Learning to cook smart, healthful dishes will benefit you for the rest of your life, whether you're still cooking our recipes or not. When you eat real food, you give your body the building blocks it needs to create the best version of you. We're gonna start slow. We want you to be excited about your meals, even though it can feel like a slog to start cooking. We know that often the fastest food, regardless of its healthfulness, is a kind of mercy when you can't be bothered to make one.more.goddamn. decision. Let us help. We've been doing this cooking thing for a long time, and we've got plenty of tricks to help you have a better relationship with food. Stick with us and soon you'll be able to whip up a fast, healthy-ish meal without even thinking about it. Fast doesn't have to mean flavorless.

If you consider cooking a soul-sucking, almost optional chore, then naturally you're gonna hate this shit forever. But that's just your perspective, and it could use an adjustment. Cooking food for yourself and anyone else is an act of love. When you do it for yourself, not only are you emphatically prioritizing your needs—what tastes good to you and what you need to feel satiated—but you're also giving yourself resources for a better life. You can build a world where you run on mystery meats and artificial colors, or you can plan for a future full of all the vitamins and minerals that come from real fucking food made by you. You're preparing something delicious that will fuel you and the people you love. And the more you cook, particularly with us by your side, that shit is just gonna get easier and easier. Plus, you've been making that same dump-and-stir casserole for how long now?

Sounds like your palate could use a goddamn vacation.

You owe it to yourself and all the delicious food you've never tasted before to give cooking a real try.

We believe that real, everyday cooking shouldn't be hard. Weeknight meals shouldn't take Herculean efforts of prep on Sundays or hours in the kitchen to get made. Who the fuck has that many storage containers anyway? No one wants to eat leftovers from the same motherfucking meal four days in a row either. We hate how cooking for

yourself has become something people think you need days of planning to pull off. All these common cooking hacks do is turn you into a joyless kitchen assembly worker and take all the fun out of eating. On average, people today spend half as much time in the kitchen as a generation ago. That's why grandma could whip up dinner in 30 minutes with whatever the fuck was in the fridge. SHE HAD PRACTICE. We understand that most of us have barely any time to begin with. Our schedules are fucking packed from dawn 'til dusk. That's why all our recipes for weekday foods take less than 45 minutes to make, start to finish. Yup, from chopping to chomping. We want everything you make to be bringing you some sort of healthy something, but at the end of the day the food needs to be craveable and practical.

The longer weekend recipes are just as important to building your skills in the kitchen as their faster brethren. Grandma could cook fast because first she learned to cook slow, you know? When you block out time in the kitchen to cook some longer recipes, you learn so many tricks that will make you a faster cook when pressed for time. You can perfect your stovetop multitasking, your chopping techniques, your mise en place all without looking at the clock or someone in your family crying about how late dinner is. When you get confident at cooking slowly, then it's no big deal to speed that shit up. You never know when hunger will come knocking, so those skills have gotta stay sharp.

So you're on board, but we can feel your hesitation about eating so many plants. We get it. Most of us grew up with broccoli, salads, and beans that were cooked with open hostility. They all tasted like shit because no one took the time to learn how to season and cook them properly. Vegetables, like anything we eat, are only as good as you make them. We've all had terrible, bland chicken and dry-as-fuck pork chops, but somehow, we don't blame meat for that, just the cook. Well lucky for you, we've been cooking exclusively vegan meals for over twenty years so we have all the know-how you need to make your meals so fucking delicious you'll forget you ever hated to cook. The fact that these dishes are more healthful than your average meal will help you keep the momentum going when all the fake fluff you're used to eating would have let you down. In fact, you might have noticed that none of our books calls for any ingredients like this. Sure, some are fucking delicious, but that's not how we like to cook. We use minimally processed, accessible ingredients because they're both cheaper and better for you.

Eat that fake shit when you're out in the world, but when you're cooking with us, you're cooking some motherfucking plants.

Our Story

There's no need to debate the merits of a vegan diet for your health, the planet, and slowing climate collapse. The science is in. At this point, trying to convince people to eat vegan is like getting people to wear a seatbelt. If you've got some fucking sense, you're on board. The number of people who identify as vegan worldwide has increased by over 600% since our first book dropped in 2014. More and more people try to eat plant-based meals several times a week. We know choosing what to eat takes work. How and what you eat is a deeply personal choice, whether you're vegan or not. Cultural baggage, religious practices, and family history winnow out what we put on our plate long before personal preference does. Changing your relationship with food and altering your diet doesn't happen overnight. In fact, we didn't start out as vegans either.

Michelle

I grew up where the Sacramento–San Joaquin River Delta meets San Francisco Bay. Because I'm from the Bay Area, people assume that I was surrounded by hippies and granola at every turn. Nope. Vegetarians might have lived in the city, but in my part of the working-class East Bay, it was all carne asada and BBQ. My house was no different, but I was. With both my parents working, meals were full of instant rice and whatever had been defrosted in the morning. I pushed pieces of meat around on my plate night after night, trying to hide them in my napkin. As soon as I understood the concept of "meat," I no longer wanted any part of it. The clean-plate rule had no exceptions for budding moral convictions though. My family worked hard to get that food on the table, and they expected me to eat all of it.

My habit of anthropomorphizing every single thing made meals difficult. I couldn't watch a movie or read a book with animals as the protagonists and then eat them for dinner. I had just spent hours empathizing with these animal characters, projecting all my emotions about growing up onto their struggles for agency. I related to Ariel the mermaid as much as Babe the pig. My mom was annoyed—understandably. The cognitive dissonance required to turn off my active imagination didn't come easily. Eventually, with my parents worn down from the constant battle, I got to be vegetarian and cook for myself when dinner didn't line up with my new requirements. That's how I learned my way around the kitchen as a kid.

I went vegan when I left home in 2003. I was the only one I knew. Once I understood how animals are treated in all stages and situations of our industrial food system, it didn't make sense to only stop eating them and not their by-products. People thought I was nuts. I can't watch any animal cruelty videos or even nature documentaries because I get so emotional watching animals get scared or hurt. If I can't handle that, then I can't justify

MICHELLE

MATT & TUSCON

consuming products that require animals to experience that stuff, whether I'm there to see it or not. I think that's a good metric for everyone to use. This sensitive, empathic streak used to feel embarrassing, but now I don't give a fuck. Life is hard, and I'm not trying to make shit harder for myself or any other animals who happen to share this planet with me. It's that simple. I've been vegan so long that I can't imagine any other way to be. Along the way, I learned

how to cook delicious meals with everyday ingredients because otherwise there was nothing for me eat. My endless hunger has filled the pages of these cookbooks with all the recipes I've dreamed up over my many decades eating plants.

Matt

Howdy, motherfuckers. That's right, I'm from Texas. The land of oil barons, cowboys, and football. I spent weekends as a kid on my grandparents' homestead walking the fence line and learning how to hunt. BBQ, Tex-Mex, and Dr Pepper were my dietary foundations, the Holy Trinity of a south Texas plate lunch. My family didn't cook much during the week when I was growing up. My parents both worked long hours, so frozen dinners or boxed mac and cheese with bits of sausage were typical dinners. In college, I kept up this style of eating, occasionally adding proteins, veggies, and spices to jazz up ramen noodles. I thought this was how everyone ate. I couldn't identify a cremini mushroom or dice an onion to save my life. I could assemble dinner, but I couldn't cook.

I dropped outta college and moved to California shortly after losing my mom. When she was my age, she somehow moved to LA from Texas and lived a kickass life with no money, so I said fuck it, I'll try that. Having to adapt to a new city and a job with brutal hours meant that food fell even further down my ladder of priorities. I ate whatever I could whenever I could find the time. Most meals were fried, and energy drinks constantly coursed through my veins. After a while, I started suffering debilitating acid reflux. My doctor promptly wrote me a prescription—no conversation about diet or lifestyle. I didn't like facing the inevitability of aging in my mid-twenties. I was too young to take pills to protect me from my diet, and that forced me to take a hard look at the crap I was putting in my body. Lucky for me, I had recently met Michelle, who was not only vegan but an incredible cook.

Veganism was foreign to me, and to be honest, I was afraid of becoming one of those malnourished-lookin' motherfuckers we so often associate with vegan diets. But I felt like crap and was willing to try almost anything. Eating more vegetables and cutting the processed crap wasn't as big of a deal as it seemed in my head. Not only did I not look malnourished, but my body felt better than ever after I finally gave it real nutrition. Imagine that. I stopped taking the pills almost immediately. I recovered from workouts faster, I slept better. Life improved at every margin. It's been easy to maintain all these years because I feel fucking great. Even more, my relationship with food drastically improved after starting to cook for myself and knowing exactly what was going on my plate. So now, when people ask why I'm vegan, I ask them why they're not.

How to Use This Book

If you've been cooking from our website or our books for years, you probably know your way around a kitchen. But this book has some hidden features we wanna draw your attention to, regardless of how seasoned of a cook you are. Sure, you could just flip to whatever page and start whipping something up, but we really want you to get your money's worth—even if you checked this out from the library. We busted our asses on this for y'all and want you to take advantage of everything we packed in here.

Weekdays vs. Weekends

Like most cookbooks, ours is divided into chapters based on the type of recipes in each one. The recipes in each chapter are further divided into two categories: weekday recipes and weekend recipes. The weekday recipes are in the front half of each chapter and are marked with an icon (see list on opposite page). These are the fastest recipes in the book with each taking take less than 45 minutes to make from start to finish. That's the average delivery time for food from all the big apps, so you can be sure that those recipes are AT LEAST as fast as delivery. Plus, your food will be warm when it gets to your table unlike those soggy fucking fries you ordered. Each recipe will have the approximate full cooking time written down, too, so you'll know exactly how far away dinner is when you start chopping.

The weekend recipes in the second half of each chapter are marked by an icon as well. These recipes take a little longer and involve more prep, making them ideal for days when you can afford to spend some more time in the kitchen. These recipes are great for honing specific cooking skills that will make your weekday recipes come together even faster. They also have an approximate cook time listed next to them, so you'll know if you need to clear your schedule for the afternoon, like for our Chocolate Raspberry Babka (page 211), or if you just need to focus for a little over an hour, à la our White Bean Soup with Rolled Herb Dumplings (page 131).

Each recipe will also have icons (see opposite page) to let you know if it is gluten-free, uses pantry staples, is freezer-friendly, and/or is good for leftovers.

Just a heads-up: The recipes we've marked as gluten-free are (1) entirely gluten-free or (2) easily made gluten-free by using a gluten-free item in place of the obvious gluten-filled ingredient. For example, our recipe for BBQ Mango Jackfruit Sammies (page 84) is marked as gluten-free because all you need to do is grab a gluten-free bun. Got it? Good.

We've also got all the recipes listed by their respective icons at the back of the book, so if you know you wanna make something gluten-free, you don't need to go searching each page for an icon; just head to page 232. We've got a guide on how to build your pantry on page 223 so

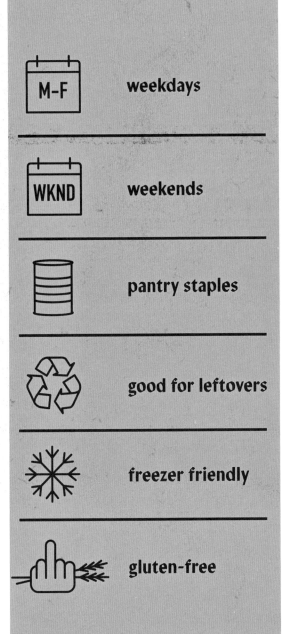

weekdays

weekends

pantry staples

good for leftovers

freezer friendly

gluten-free

that you can make the best use of those pantry staples recipes and always have the ingredients you need to cook at home. Right before that, on page 219, we've got a guide on how to cook lots of basic grains like rice and farro, as well as our favorite ways to cook some basic grocery store veggies. That way, you can mix and match or throw together a quick side, cook random veggies without a proper recipe, and get some hot tips and general cooking info whenever you need it.

We've got tons of cooking advice throughout the book, but we've highlighted the best stuff in our Cheat Sheet callouts. These tips will help you take your cooking to the next level and are featured on little notecards throughout the book so keep your eyes peeled. You'll also find Field Guide features in these pages, which are ingredient guides or more detailed advice on some shit we've learned over our decades in the kitchen. Like the Cheat Sheets, they're scattered throughout the book and accompany a specific recipe. Be sure to read those motherfuckers. They'll make you a better, more informed cook. And ultimately, that's our goal. We want you cooking and vibing with all your ingredients, regardless of whether you're using our book or your own beautiful brain.

You might stumble upon an ingredient in some of our recipes that you've never heard of or don't know where to get it. Don't panic.

Hey! Listen to us. Don't panic. K?

We've thrown together our WTF section on page 221 to define all those potentially new-to-you ingredients, tell you why we love them, and where you can find them. We didn't include these ingredients just to flex our kitchen creativity, but because they impart something special to each meal we use them in. We decided you and the dish couldn't do without them. So don't be scared; try them out, and take yourself on a taste adventure.

Finally, we've included a Meal Manager (page 230) to help you create a game plan for your week's cooking. We've included dishes that flow into one another so that you can have a great week of meals with minimal cooking and leftovers that you'll actually look forward to. There's nothing worse than eating the same meal, no matter how delicious, for five days straight. That's how you fall back into the open arms of expensive delivery apps, and we're trying to get away from that life, right? Right.

Set Up for Success

Once you've flipped through the book and picked out some recipes that've caught your attention, it's time to start cooking. Before firing up the stove though, read the recipe all the way through so you know exactly what the fuck you're diving into. We cannot stress this shit enough:

Read them all. The. Way. Through.

It only takes a couple minutes, and it will save you at least one panic attack. If you don't read the recipe, you might not realize that you need to let something rise for 2 hours and will be fucked when it comes time to eat and that shit isn't ready. Never cook hangry. We've been there and wouldn't recommend it. Mistakes get made.

Once you know what you're in for, lay out any pots, utensils, and tools that you're gonna need to whip up the recipe. It's a pain in the ass to reach for your big soup pot when you've already chopped everything and realize you loaned it to your sister last weekend and haven't gotten that shit back. Next, make sure you have all the ingredients you need. Seriously. All the spices, all the sauces, all of it. Last-minute substitutions made in a hurry usually fuck up a dish and ruin all your hard work. Don't come crying to us because you thought adding strawberry jam to your soup instead of tomato paste would work because they're both fruit. We didn't do that disgusting shit, you did. Own it. Just think it through and double-check your ingredients list before you start just dumping whatthefuckever into a bowl. You'll end up wasting food and your own damn time otherwise. But maybe you're in the kitchen exclusively for the drama. If so, continue. No further instructions are required.

Remember that this is *your* book. Dog-ear it, write in the margins, scratch out the measurements, and add your own. Use it however you want. These are recipes we've collected to help you become great home cooks who don't rely on recipes to make every meal. We want you cooking from scratch ASAP, so consider this book as your training wheels.

Now go practice.

Rise Dine

Breakfast, Brunch, and Any-Time Treats

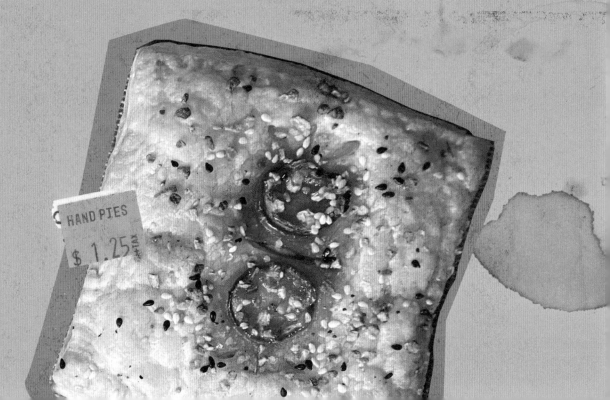

HAND PIES
$ 1.25 +TAX

Everyday Tofu Scramble

The best and worst thing about tofu is that it has very little flavor. That means when it comes to seasoning, you need to bring it. Bland tofu is always the cook's fault, not the tofu's. We love this scramble because it has tons of fucking flavor for very little work AND most people won't even know it's tofu. Don't tell them until they ask where you get your protein from. Then turn to them slowly and softly say, "Hopefully you." They'll immediately bail, and you'll get this scramble all to yourself.

1 tablespoon olive oil

¼ onion or 1 shallot, finely chopped

1 package (14 ounces) extra-firm tofu

1 tablespoon Bragg Liquid Aminos, soy sauce, or tamari

2 tablespoons nutritional yeast (nooch)

½ teaspoon garlic powder

½ teaspoon paprika or chili powder

¼ teaspoon ground turmeric (optional), for color

1 carrot, shredded on a box grater

Salt and pepper or everything bagel seasoning

Chopped fresh herbs like chives, dill, or cilantro (optional)

1 Warm the oil in a large sauté pan over medium heat. Add the onion and cook until it starts to soften, 2 to 3 minutes. While the onion is cooking, drain the tofu and squeeze out any extra liquid with your hands. Next, take your hands and crush the tofu, tearing it into bite-size bits and squeezing it through your fingers right into the hot pan. There's no wrong way to do this shit. Just make sure the tofu is in small crumbles.

2 Mix the crumbled tofu with the cooked onion, then drizzle with the liquid aminos and stir to combine. Next, sprinkle the tofu with the nooch, garlic powder, paprika, and turmeric (if using). Let this cook, stirring occasionally, until the tofu firms up a little and doesn't feel so soft when you move it around the pan, 2 to 4 minutes. Fold in the shredded carrots and season with salt and pepper or everything bagel seasoning to taste. Cook for a minute more, just long enough for the carrots to wilt, you know?

3 If you want, garnish with fresh herbs. Serve right away.

CHEAT SHEET:

We love this as an everyday breakfast with some toast, fresh tomato, and avocado, if we've got it. But if you want to do a big brunch spread, these pair great with our Poblano Home Fries (page 38), Red Pepper Rice (page 110), Everyday Cabbage Slaw (page 67), and some tortillas. Known tofu hater in the house? Try grating the tofu with the same side of the box grater that you used for the carrot. This will give your scramble a finer, less obvious tofu texture.

Breakfast Fried Rice

This dish makes for a quick and easy breakfast but tastes like you spent hours in the kitchen. The only trick is that you MUST use leftover, cold rice. You cannot—HEY, PAY THE FUCK ATTENTION—absolutely CANNOT make fried rice with warm, freshly cooked rice. It'll just turn to mush. Embrace leftovers.

1 tablespoon neutral oil, such as plain, unroasted peanut oil

1 shallot or ¼ white onion, minced

1 carrot, diced

2¼ cups cold leftover cooked rice, like jasmine or brown rice

2 tablespoons rice vinegar

2 tablespoons tamari or soy sauce

1 garlic clove, grated or minced

1 teaspoon toasted sesame oil

¼ cup minced chives or green onions

Hemp or sesame seeds, for topping (optional)

Fresh tomatoes and avocado, for serving

Salt and black pepper

1 Grab a wok or a large sauté pan and warm the oil over medium-high heat. Add the shallot and carrot and cook them just until the shallot starts to look translucent, 3 to 4 minutes. Now add the rice and mix it all together. If the rice looks a little dry and is hard to stir, splash a tablespoon or two of water in the pan until you can break up the cold rice.

2 Once the rice starts to warm up and is easy to sauté around, drizzle with the vinegar and tamari. Toss the rice around so every grain gets some love, 1 to 2 minutes. Add the garlic and sesame oil and cook for about a minute more, just so the garlic isn't raw as hell. Fold in the chives and taste. Add whatever you think it needs, then remove from the heat.

3 Serve warm. If you want, garnish with hemp or sesame seeds. We love to top the bowl off with a sliced fresh tomato, a couple pieces of avocado, and a little salt and pepper.

Breakfast Blender Sammies

We love how easy breakfast can be with all the faux egg products out there, but we don't love all the random, highly processed ingredients in them. Our bodies deserve better. Here's a recipe for your own egg substitute that's just as fucking easy to use and super delicious.

Batter

1 block (12 ounces) extra-firm silken tofu*

¼ cup nondairy milk

2 tablespoons olive oil

1 tablespoon ume plum vinegar or Bragg Liquid Aminos

¼ cup nutritional yeast (nooch)

2 tablespoons cornstarch

2 tablespoons chickpea flour

2 teaspoons garlic powder

1 teaspoon paprika

½ teaspoon ground turmeric

Salt and pepper

Sammies

Spray oil

8 slices toasted bread

Sliced tomatoes and avocados, for serving

Sriracha Aioli (see Tofu Mayo Cheat Sheet, page 95)

*You want the kind of silken tofu that's shelf-stable, not the stuff packed in water.

1 Make the batter: Grab your blender and throw in the tofu, milk, olive oil, plum vinegar, nooch, cornstarch, chickpea flour, garlic powder, paprika, turmeric, and a pinch each of salt and pepper. Run that shit until it looks super smooth in there. Blender not blending? Add another tablespoon or two of milk until you get it to run. If you have to add more than ¼ cup of liquid, (1) get a new fucking blender, and (2) add another tablespoon of cornstarch so that it doesn't get too runny.

2 Cook the sammies: Grab a small skillet or sauté pan and heat it over medium-high heat. Spray the pan lightly with a little oil and pour in about ½ cup of the batter. Cook on one side until it starts to thicken and brown in spots, 2 to 3 minutes. Flip and cook until it's browned on the other side, too. Repeat until you use all of the batter.

3 Serve right away between some toasty bread slathered with fresh tomatoes and avocado, and our Sriracha aioli.

CHEAT SHEET:

Hosting brunch? Make this with a baguette. Let people dip the baguette slices into the salsa or set them on a tray like bruschetta. It's painfully easy. People will think you're so fucking clever, it'll be borderline annoying how impressed they are.

Savory Green Onion Toasts with Fresh Tomato Salsa

Avocado toast is out. Now begins the reign of battered bread topped with fresh salsa. Adjust your personality accordingly.

¼ cup chickpea flour

2 tablespoons cornstarch

1 tablespoon nutritional yeast (nooch)

1 teaspoon garlic powder

¼ teaspoon black pepper

1 cup nondairy milk

¼ cup minced green onions or chives

8 slices crusty bread, no thicker than ½ inch, like sourdough

Nondairy butter, for serving

Fresh Tomato Salsa (recipe follows)

1 Mix the chickpea flour, cornstarch, nooch, garlic powder, and black pepper together in a shallow bowl. Whisk in the milk until there are no chunks floating around in there and set that shit aside for about 10 minutes. It's gonna thicken up as it sits so you might as well make the tomato salsa now.

2 Once the mixture has thickened up, stir in the minced green onions. The batter is complete, congrats. Warm up a griddle over medium-high heat. Dunk your slices of bread two at a time into the batter, letting them sit in there for at least a minute, before flipping and letting them sit for 30 seconds more. The green onions will kinda sink to the bottom so make sure to scoop some of them up and spread them across the top of the bread as you pull them out. Place the battered bread on the hot griddle and cook until they're browned and crispy, 1 to 2 minutes a side, depending on your stove. Flip and repeat that shit. Keep going until all your toasts are crispy. You can freeze them just like this and warm them up in the toaster oven or under the low setting of your broiler, just as you would frozen French toast.

3 Serve hot, slathered in butter, and topped with the fresh tomato salsa (or simply a tomato slice with salt if you're in a rush).

(recipe continues)

Fresh Tomato Salsa

Makes 1½ cups / Cook time: 5 minutes

2 fist-size tomatoes, chopped

1 shallot or ¼ red onion, minced

2 tablespoons sliced green onions

1 tablespoon fresh lemon juice

1 tablespoon rice vinegar

Pinch of salt

Mix the tomatoes, shallot, green onions, lemon juice, rice vinegar, and salt together until everything looks incorporated. Done. Painless, right?

Breakfast Bean Bowls

This isn't so much a recipe as it is a reminder that beans and rice are a fucking killer breakfast. If you make our Sunday Beans (page 155), you should have these ready to go whenever you need a quick breakfast during the week. This is a great place to use up random leftovers like roasted veggies or Our Everyday Cabbage Slaw (page 67).

1½ cups Sunday Beans (page 155) or 1 can (15 ounces) beans (drained, rinsed, and seasoned with salt and pepper), warmed up

1 cup cooked rice

1 avocado, sliced

1 tomato, sliced

Salt

4 corn tortillas, warmed

Handful of fresh cilantro, chopped

1 lime, halved

Divide the beans and rice evenly between two low-rimmed bowls. Place half of the avocado and tomato slices on the side with a pinch of salt. Add the warmed tortillas to the side of the bowl, top the whole thing with some cilantro, and place a lime half right in the bowl next to the tortillas. Serve right away.

CHEAT SHEET:

Want to make this breakfast bowl a whole gourmet thing? Choose any of these optional add-ins and toss them right into the bowl next to beans:
- Poblano Home Fries (page 38)
- Cumin Rice (page 115)
- Red Pepper Rice (page 110)
- Everyday Cabbage Slaw (page 67)
- Grilled Plantains (page 99)

Top it off with either sauce:
- Grilled Tomatillo and Avocado Salsa (page 108)
- Cilantro Chimichurri (page 100)

Morning Cornbread

Cornbread isn't strictly a breakfast food, but it's a damn fine way to start your day. Don't let the carbs fool you—cornmeal is rich in fiber and phosphorus. And did we mention the versatility? The leftovers go great with dinner. Try it as a side to our Sunday Beans (page 155) or with a soup like our Farro and Red Bean Soup (page 120).

Nondairy butter and flour, for the pan

1 cup cornmeal*

1 cup whole wheat pastry or all-purpose flour**

3 tablespoons brown sugar

2 teaspoons baking powder

½ teaspoon baking soda

½ teaspoon salt

1¾ cups nondairy milk

3 tablespoons melted nondairy butter or olive oil

2 tablespoons ground flaxseeds

1 teaspoon apple cider vinegar

Nondairy butter and/or jam, for serving (optional)

*Try to grab a bag that says it's for baking or cornbread or one with cornmeal that looks closer to flour than it does to polenta.

**The nuttiness of the whole wheat pastry flour complements the cornmeal really nicely. It's a great place to use this more nutritious flour.

1 Warm your oven up to 425°F. Grease and flour an 8 × 8-inch baking pan, like what you'd make brownies in.

2 Grab a large bowl and whisk together the cornmeal, flour, brown sugar, baking powder, baking soda, and salt. In a smaller bowl, stir together the milk, melted butter, ground flaxseeds, and vinegar. Pour the milk mixture into the flour mixture and mix them up until they're *just* combined.

3 Now scrape all that into your prepared baking pan and stick it in the oven until a toothpick stuck into the center comes out smooth, 20 to 25 minutes.

4 Let the cornbread cool for a couple minutes before you start clawing into it like a bunch of animals. Cut into 9 squares. For breakfast, we love this cornbread as is or smothered in jam or your favorite nondairy butter. Cornbread also freezes like a dream so either slip some squares into a freezer bag or double the recipe and freeze the extra cornbread. Take the cornbread squares out of the freezer and let them thaw in your fridge overnight or use your microwave to get it done faster.

CHEAT SHEET:

Want to turn our morning cornbread into a grab-and-go food? Make it into muffins. Heat up the oven to 350°F. Line the 12 cups of a standard muffin tin with paper liners or grease and flour each muffin well. Spoon the batter evenly into the prepared cups, filling each cup about three-quarters full so that shit doesn't overflow. Bake until the tops look golden, 13 to 15 minutes. These muffins freeze great, too. Just store them in an airtight bag or container in the freezer for up to 3 months.

Savory Breakfast Hand Pies

This recipe is more of a guidepost to show you how to make hand pies for a week-long mobile meal. Treat these fillings as options—you can do whatever the fuck you want. Think of this as a choose-your-own breakfast adventure.

Quick Homemade Puff Pastry (recipe follows) or 2 sheets of store-bought puff pastry

Everyday Tofu Scramble (page 20)

Queso Blanco (page 96)

2 tablespoons nondairy milk

2 tablespoons olive oil

Sesame seeds, everything bagel seasoning, or thinly sliced jalapeños, for topping

1 Roll out your puff pastry blocks into 2 equal-size sheets. You want each sheet to be about the size of a sheet of paper. Cut each sheet into a grid of identical rectangles, aiming for 9 small rectangles for each sheet (18 rectangles in total).

2 In a medium bowl, combine the tofu scramble and 1 cup of the queso until everything looks evenly mixed.

3 Line a large baking sheet with parchment paper. Grab three squares of the puff pastry at a time and place them in front of you. Put no more than ¼ cup of the filling mixture in the center of each rectangle. Wet the edges of the puff pastry with your finger, then place then place three more rectangles of puff pastry on top of the prepared ones and press down the edges. Place the finished hand pies on the lined baking sheet. Keep going until you run out of puff pastry. You should have 9 hand pies.

4 Throw the baking sheet with the hand pies into the freezer, if you have room, for 15 minutes while you clean up. No room? Place them in a cool spot or in the fridge. This cooler temp will help them hold their shape better as they bake.

5 When the hand pies are almost done chilling, warm up your oven to 400°F.

(recipe continues)

6 Cut one or two vents in the top of each hand pie so that any steam or queso goo can come out without fucking up your sealed edges. Mix the milk and the oil in a small glass and brush that on top of the hand pies. Now you can sprinkle over sesame seeds, everything bagel seasoning, some thinly sliced jalapeños, or whatever you're into. Place them in the oven and bake until they look nice and golden brown, 20 to 25 minutes.

7 Let the hand pies cool for 15 minutes before serving. Set the remaining queso out as a dipping sauce. The baked hand pies can be stored in the freezer for up to 3 months. To reheat, bake the hand pies at 350°F for 10 to 15 minutes.

Quick Homemade Puff Pastry

Makes 2 sheets /
Cook time: 2½ hours, mostly inactive

2½ sticks (10 ounces) cold nondairy butter

2 cups all-purpose flour

¼ teaspoon salt

½ cup cold water

Don't let the length of the instructions make you think this shit isn't easy. The hardest part is rolling the dough out and folding it, which honestly isn't fucking hard at all. But describing that process is hard, which is why the directions are so long. Do you need to make your own puff pastry? Fuck no. But should you make it at least once so that you truly understand how much fat is in there? Fuck yes.

1 Cut the butter into dice-size cubes and throw them in the freezer for 15 minutes. This will get the cubes nice and cold.

2 When the 15 minutes are almost up, grab your food processor and dump the flour and salt in there. Dump half the cold butter into the food processor and pulse until the butter almost disappears into the flour. Add the rest of the butter and pulse a few more times until just combined, like max 5 pulses more. Yes, there are still giant chunks of butter but chill, we're not done. Lastly, drizzle the cold water over the flour mixture and then pulse 5 more times until a rough dough comes together. Some remaining big chunks of butter are fine. They'll help the pastry get nice and flaky.

3 Dump the dough onto a lightly floured surface and knead it a few times until you can shape it into a square when you sorta pat it together. If the dough seems a little dry, wet your hands and press it together. You want the least amount of water in this dough as you can get away with, so don't fuck around with it too much. The heat from your hands will also start to melt all those butter chunks, and we don't want that. SO DO THE LEAST, K?

4 Grab your rolling pin and roll the square out to about the size of a standard half-sheet pan, which is about 18 × 13 inches (A). Now you need to think back to elementary school when your teacher taught you all how to fold. Place a short end of the dough closest to you and fold it up, hamburger-style, halfway up the dough. Fold the remaining dough over the same way so that both the short ends meet in the middle of the dough (B).

(recipe continues)

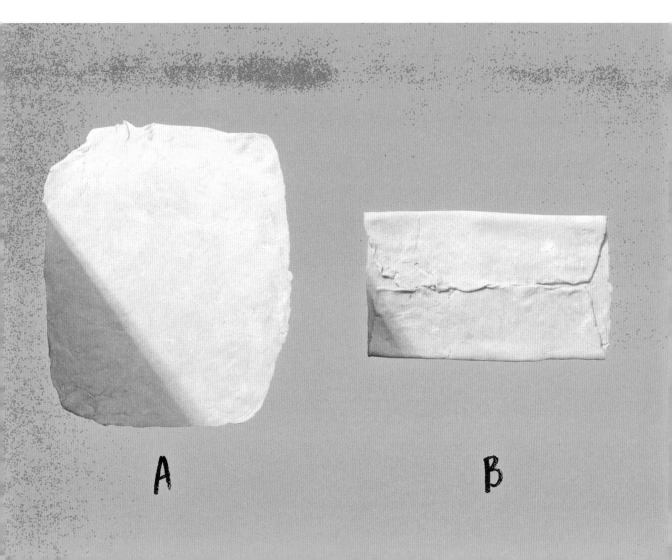

A

B

5 Fold this again in half again, hamburger-style so that you have a long envelope-shaped piece of dough with four layers (C). Now fold it in half, hot-dog style, so that the remaining shape is similar to a greeting card (D). Cut that shit in half so that each piece has part of the last folded edge (E), wrap the halves with plastic wrap, and stick them in the fridge. All those folds are the key to having flaky layers, so congrats, the hardest part is behind you.

6 Let that chill in the fridge for at least 1½ hours before using. It will keep in the fridge for 3 days, but if you throw it in the freezer, tightly wrapped, it will be good for about 3 months. To use after chilling in the fridge, roll the dough out on a well-floured surface and follow the rest of your recipe's instructions. To use from the freezer, place the frozen dough in the fridge and let it thaw overnight before treating it like freshly made dough.

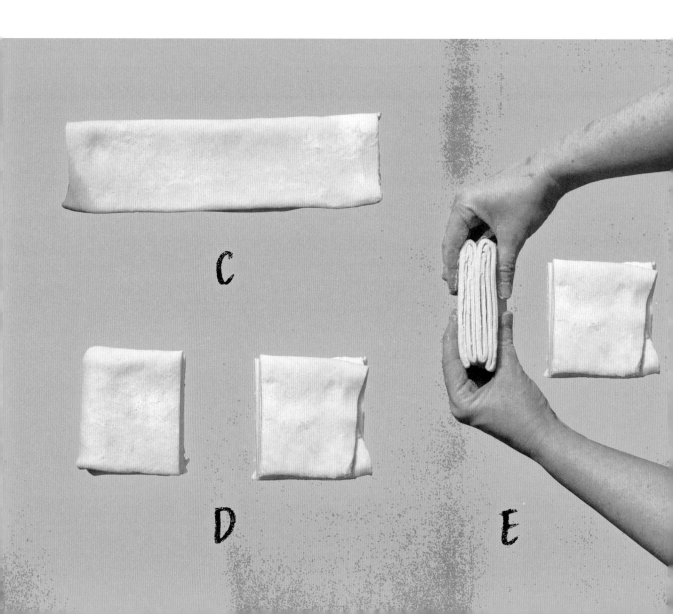

C

D

E

FIELD GUIDE:
HAND PIE HANDBOOK

Hand pies are a great way to use up leftovers and make an easy breakfast for times when you just can't do one more fucking thing. Here are ideas for some more filling combos using recipes in these pages so you can turn anything you didn't totally demolish into a hand pie, no matter what you wanna eat. Just remember that each one only needs about ¼ cup of filling, so don't overload them. Enjoy any leftover filling as the hand pies bake. You're welcome.

LOADED BREAKFAST HAND PIES
- EVERYDAY TOFU SCRAMBLE (PAGE 20)
- POBLANO HOME FRIES (PAGE 38)
- QUESO BLANCO (PAGE 96)

SUMMER SQUASH HAND PIES
- FILLING FROM SUMMER SQUASH–STUFFED FLATBREAD (PAGE 147)
- TAHINI CUCUMBER SAUCE (OPTIONAL; PAGE 93), FOR DIPPING

WINTER SQUASH HAND PIES
- BAKED BUTTERNUT SQUASH (PAGE 166), PUREED WITH JUST ENOUGH BROTH TO RUN THE BLENDER
- 1 CUP TOMATO LENTIL SAUCE (FROM BAKED BUTTERNUT SQUASH, PAGE 166)
- GARLIC-MINT YOGURT (OPTIONAL; PAGE 94), FOR DIPPING

PLANTAIN AND BEAN HAND PIES
- 2 GRILLED PLANTAINS (PAGE 99), MASHED UP
- ½ BATCH CHEATER BEANS (PAGE 138)
- CILANTRO CHIMICHURRI (OPTIONAL; PAGE 100), FOR DIPPING

To freeze, place the cooked hand pies on a baking sheet and put them in the freezer for at least 1 hour. Once frozen, you can throw all the hand pies together in an airtight bag or container, and they'll keep for 3 months in the freezer. To thaw, place them in the oven or toaster oven at 300°F until the puff pastry is crispy and the filling is warm, 10 to 15 minutes.

Makes enough for 4 people / Cook time: 1 hour, mostly inactive

Poblano Home Fries

We love potatoes in every single form, but home fries have a special place in our hearts. If you can't find a poblano, feel free to sub in a bell pepper or leave it out, if you're not into them. We think they add a great taste and texture, but what the fuck do we know? We've only written five cookbooks.

3 russet or large Yukon Gold potatoes, peeled or not, chopped into pieces no larger than a nickel

½ yellow onion, chopped

1 poblano pepper, chopped

2 tablespoons olive oil

2 teaspoons chili powder

½ teaspoon salt

1 teaspoon ground cumin

¼ teaspoon black pepper

4 garlic cloves, minced

1 tablespoon fresh lime juice

1 tablespoon ume plum vinegar (optional)

1 Place the chopped potatoes in a bowl and cover them with water. Stir them around with your fingers for a minute to help them release some of their excess starch. This will make the potatoes crispier, which is all anyone wants in life. Let them chill in the water while you prep the rest of the ingredients.

2 Warm up your oven to 425°F.

3 Drain and rinse the potatoes, then dump them into a large bowl along with the onion and poblano. Drizzle with the olive oil and toss so that everything is coated in some oil. In a small bowl, mix together the chili powder, salt, cumin, and black pepper. Sprinkle the spices over the vegetables, then toss that shit around until everything looks covered. Spread this mixture onto a sheet pan in an even layer and place it in the oven.

4 Bake until the potatoes look a little crispy and golden brown in some places, 30 to 40 minutes, stirring halfway to make sure everything is getting roasted. In the last 5 minutes of cooking, add the garlic, lime juice, and plum vinegar. Stir and continue roasting. Let the potatoes cool for a few minutes before serving. Taste and add more salt or whatever the fuck you think they need.

Fall Sheet Pan Hash Browns

This giant hash brown is the stuff that dreams are made of. Or at least our dreams.

3 cups grated peeled russet potatoes (about 2 medium)

½ cup grated carrot (about 2 carrots)

½ cup grated parsnip (about 1 parsnip)

3 tablespoons olive oil

2 teaspoons no-salt, all-purpose seasoning blend

½ teaspoon garlic powder

½ teaspoon salt, plus more for sprinkling

¼ cup panko bread crumbs

2 tablespoons nutritional yeast (nooch)

1 Warm up your oven to 400°F. Line your sheet pan with some parchment paper.

2 Add the potatoes, carrot, and parsnip to a bowl and toss to combine. Fill that bowl with water and swish everything around for a couple minutes. Drain and repeat the process. This will make the hash browns crispy. Rinse the potato mixture in a colander under cold water and let them drip off as much water as possible.

3 While they're drying, mix together the olive oil, all-purpose seasoning, garlic powder, and salt in a small bowl. In another little bowl, mix together the panko and nooch.

4 Dry off any water from the potato mixture and the bowl with a clean kitchen towel. Toss the mixture back into the dried-off bowl. Pour in the olive oil mixture and toss until everything looks coated. Sprinkle in the panko mixture and toss again until everything looks uniformly mixed.

5 Spread the potato mixture out on the sheet pan in a single, even layer. Some overlap is fine but the thinner the layer, the crispier the hash brown. Don't overcrowd that shit.

6 Bake until the edges are starting to look crispy and brown, about 25 minutes. Want the top to be extra crispy? Throw them under your broiler on high for an additional 2 to 5 minutes, watching it closely. To serve, cut the baked potatoes into individual servings. Sprinkle with salt and serve hot.

Makes enough for 4 to 6 people /
Cook time: 40 minutes, mostly inactive

Red Chilaquiles

For anyone who has never had chilaquiles, welcome to the first day of the rest of your fucking life. Eating nachos for breakfast is kinda frowned upon. Chilaquiles are not only a great way to use stale tortillas from the night before but also a breakfast nacho work-around. This recipe uses dried chiles, which you can find in the spice section or produce section of your grocery story or, you know, online.

16 to 20 corn tortillas

Red Sauce

4 Roma tomatoes

2 cups vegetable broth

½ white onion

2 dried guajillo chiles*

2 dried chiles de árbol*

2 garlic cloves

½ teaspoon salt

½ teaspoon dried oregano

1 tablespoon nutritional yeast (nooch)

1 tablespoon fresh lime juice

If you can't find chiles where you live, we feel sorry for you. Try subbing in 2 to 3 tablespoons of your favorite chili powder or a chili powder blend with a similar, sorta smoky flavor.

1 Warm up your oven up to 400°F.

2 Cut your tortillas up into 8 wedges each, you know, like a lil' pizza. Spread the wedges out on a baking sheet or two and throw them in the oven for 15 to 25 minutes to dry out. Stir them around halfway through. It's fine if they start to get hard in some spots, but don't let them burn. When they are all crispy, set them aside.

3 While those guys are baking, let's make the red sauce: In a small saucepan, throw together the tomatoes, vegetable broth, white onion, both chiles, and the garlic. Heat over medium-high and let it come to a rolling simmer for about 10 minutes. You want to see the chiles softening and the tomatoes bursting in their skins. If the tomatoes or onion are popping out of the broth, turn them over halfway through so that everyone gets some time in the hot broth bath.

4 After 10 minutes, remove from the heat and let the pot cool down a little. If the chiles have stems, now is a good time to grab a fork and rip them off. Once everything is cool, pour the whole pot into a blender along with the salt, oregano, nooch, and lime juice. Run the blender until that shit looks smooth. You can put this sauce in the fridge until

(recipe and ingredients continue)

CHEAT SHEET:

We were trying to cut down on the salt and fat by using tortillas, but if you wanna, you can use corn chips instead. Just grab a big-ass bag of chips and eyeball it.

For Serving

House Crema (recipe follows) or avocado

Chopped red onion

Jalapeños

Cilantro

Sunday Beans (page 155)

1 block (12 ounces) soft silken tofu*

3 tablespoons neutral oil, such as avocado oil

3 tablespoons fresh lime juice

1 garlic clove, minced

¼ teaspoon salt

***You want the kind of silken tofu that's shelf-stable, not the stuff packed in water in the cold case. You'll find it near the soy sauce at most grocery stores.**

it's breakfast time, or you can get cooking right away. This will keep for 3 days refrigerated, but it is really best within the first 24 hours it's made.

5 To make the chilaquiles, warm up the sauce in a large sauté pan or skillet over medium heat. Once it comes to a low simmer, add half the tortillas. Toss until everything is coated, then add the rest of the tortillas. Let them start to absorb in the sauce, about 2 minutes, then remove from the heat. Serve warm topped with crema or avocado, red onion, jalapeños, cilantro, and a side of Sunday beans.

House Crema

Makes about 2 cups / Cook time: 5 minutes

We like tofu as the base for our crema since it's neutral in taste and low in fat. Drizzle this crema over our Red Chilaquiles (page 40) or our Green Enchiladas (page 171), stuff it in a burrito (see Field Guide: Build a Burrito Bar, page 163), or use it as a dip for slices of Summer Squash-Stuffed Flatbread (page 147). As soon as you taste it, you'll think of a million different places to use it.

Throw everything in a blender or food processor and run that shit until it's smooth in there, about 30 seconds. Let this sit for at least 30 minutes before serving to really let the lime juice sour things up. This will keep in the fridge in a jar for about a week, but it's best within the first 3 days. If it starts to separate, just throw it back in the blender and run that shit again.

White Bean and Mushroom Breakfast Cobbler

Think biscuits and gravy but, like, elevated. Kinda like flying first class once and telling yourself you'll never fly coach again. Sure, this won't be breakfast every day, but when it is? That's a *fancy* day.

3 tablespoons olive oil

1 carrot, chopped

4 cups roughly chopped mixed mushrooms, like button, cremini, oyster, and maitake

Salt and black pepper

½ sweet onion, chopped

1 teaspoon dried thyme

1 tablespoon chopped fresh sage

3 garlic cloves, minced

1 tablespoon Bragg Liquid Aminos

2 tablespoons all-purpose flour

1½ cups cooked white beans, like cannellini or Great Northern, or 1 can (15 ounces), drained and rinsed

Biscuit Topping

¾ cup nondairy milk

1 teaspoon apple cider vinegar

1¼ cups all-purpose flour

1 Warm up your oven to 375°F.

2 In a large ovenproof skillet or braiser, heat the olive oil over medium heat. Add the carrot and mushrooms, sprinkle with some salt and pepper, and sauté, stirring occasionally, until the mushrooms begin to brown and have released most of their moisture, 8 to 10 minutes.

3 Add the onion, thyme, sage, and garlic and let that cook until the onion starts to look translucent, about 5 minutes. Drizzle in the liquid aminos, then sprinkle in the flour. Stir until everything looks well mixed and sorta like gravy. Now remove from the heat and stir in the white beans. Let this sit on the stove while you make the biscuit topping.

4 Make the biscuit topping: In a glass, mix the milk and vinegar together and set it aside. In a large bowl, whisk together the flour, sugar, baking powder, baking soda, and salt. Dump in the butter and with your fingers, rub the butter into the flour mixture until it resembles coarse sand. This is what melts in the oven and makes your biscuits flaky, so just be patient with this shit. It's not hard. If your butter

(recipe and ingredients continue)

2 tablespoons sugar

2 teaspoons baking powder

½ teaspoon baking soda

½ teaspoon salt

4 tablespoons cold nondairy butter or coconut oil

To Finish

1½ cups vegetable broth

Freshly cracked black pepper

is too warm and getting all melty on you, just stick the whole bowl in the freezer for 10 to 15 minutes and try again. Once all the butter is worked in, make a well in the center of the flour mixture and pour in the milk from earlier. Mix until everything is just combined.

5 Back to the mushrooms. Slowly stir the veggie broth into the mushroom mixture. This is gonna thicken up and evaporate in the oven. Trust the process. Scoop the biscuit dough and dollop the scoops on top of the mushroom mixture until you cover most of the surface or run out of dough, whatever happens first. Throw this in the oven to bake until the biscuits are golden brown, 35 to 40 minutes.

6 To serve, scoop a portion right from the pan into a bowl making sure to get all the beans and mushrooms you can. Top with fresh cracked black pepper.

Makes 9 to 12 rolls, depending on how you slice them /
Cook time: 3 hours, mostly inactive

Pumpkin Cinnamon Rolls

These would be just as home in the dessert section of the book, but something this special deserves to be shown off at a brunch, the morning after a sleepover, or the morning of someone's birthday. Any morning worth celebrating is worth celebrating with these on your plate.

Dough

1 cup nondairy milk, warmed

2 envelopes (4½ teaspoons) active dry yeast

4½ cups all-purpose flour, plus ½ cup for kneading

¼ cup cane sugar

1 teaspoon salt

½ teaspoon ground cinnamon

¼ teaspoon ground nutmeg

¼ cup unsweetened pumpkin puree, canned or homemade*

2 tablespoons olive oil

Pumpkin Filling

1¼ cups unsweetened pumpkin puree, canned or homemade*

¾ cup packed brown sugar

2 tablespoons fresh lemon juice

1 teaspoon vanilla extract

Pinch of salt

¼ cup melted nondairy butter or coconut oil

1 First let's make the dough: Add the yeast to the warm milk and let the yeast wake up and get foamy for about 10 minutes. If the milk is too hot, it will murder all the yeast and you'll have to start over after you throw a yeast funeral. IS THAT HOW YOU WANT TO SPEND YOUR DAY? Didn't think so. Warm the milk until you can still hold a finger in the glass comfortably. Then swirl in the yeast and move on.

2 While the yeast isn't being murdered, whisk together the 4½ cups flour, the cane sugar, salt, cinnamon, and nutmeg in a big bowl (or the bowl of your stand mixer).

3 Add the ¼ cup pumpkin puree and the olive oil to the yeast mixture and stir until everything is incorporated. Using a wooden spoon (or the dough hook of your stand mixer on low speed), stir while pouring in the yeasty pumpkin mixture. Knead the dough by hand for 10 minutes (or use the dough hook on medium speed to knead the dough for 5 minutes), adding up to an additional ½ cup flour as needed, until a soft, smooth, elastic dough forms.

4 Shape the dough into a ball and throw it in a large, greased-up bowl and cover. Let this hang out in a warm place until it's almost doubled in size, 1 to ½ hours.

5 Once the dough is almost done rising, start making the pumpkin filling: In a medium bowl, whisk together the 1¼ cups pumpkin puree, brown sugar, lemon juice, vanilla, and salt until everything looks totally combined.

⅓ cup packed brown sugar

¼ cup maple syrup

¼ cup melted nondairy butter or coconut oil

2 teaspoons vanilla extract

1 cup chopped toasted pecans (optional but you gotta love the crunch)

*Making homemade pumpkin puree isn't hard. Just peel and chop some pumpkin, then steam it until tender, about 15 minutes, or roast it at 400°F for about 25 minutes, with a little oil until you can easily pierce the pieces with a fork, depending on how large your pieces are. However you cook them, throw the tender pieces into a food processor and run that shit until there's a smooth puree in there. This tastes better than canned, we swear.

6 Punch down the dough, knead it once or twice, and place it on a well-floured surface. Roll the dough out to a 10 × 16-inch rectangle, keeping one of the long sides facing you. Brush the top with the melted butter. Evenly spread the pumpkin mixture over the dough, but leave a ½-inch border across the top and bottom long sides. Now we roll. Dip your fingertips in water and wet the border of dough on the long side farthest from you. Starting at the long side near you, roll the dough up with the filling into a long, tight burrito shape, keeping the ends open. Press the wet edge into the dough a little bit so it seals the pumpkin log shut. Is your pumpkin filling everywhere and making a mess? Stick that log in the freezer for 10 to 15 minutes to cool off and go clean your ass up.

7 Warm up the oven to 350°F. Grease and flour a standard 9 × 13-inch baking dish.

8 When the roll has firmed up a little, pull it out of the fridge and slice it crosswise into 1½- to 2-inch-thick slices, placing them cut side up in the prepared baking dish. Cover this with a clean kitchen towel and let it rise for another 30 minutes until they have almost doubled in size or, you know, look like cinnamon rolls.

9 Bake until the rolls look golden and the centers don't look raw, 20 to 25 minutes.

10 While they're baking, make the maple glaze: In a small saucepan, mix the brown sugar, maple syrup, and melted butter over medium heat. Whisk frequently until all the sugar has dissolved, then reduce the heat to medium-low. Add the vanilla and simmer the whole pot slowly, again, stirring that shit frequently, for 5 more minutes. Remove from the heat, cover, and stir every few minutes to keep a gross skin from forming.

11 When the rolls are done, let them cool for 5 to 10 minutes before glazing. Fold the chopped pecans, if using, into the glaze and mix until everything is well combined. Drizzle that sweet shit evenly over the cooked pumpkin cinnamon rolls. Let this all cool for another 10 minutes before serving. You can freeze these after baking, as a tray or individually. Just defrost them in the microwave, 45 seconds per roll.

Midd
Mun

10¢

ay chies

Sammies, Salads, and Other Light Bites

Makes enough for 4 people / Cook time: 15 minutes

Simple Side Salad with House Vinaigrette

This recipe is for when you know you need some leafy greens on your plate because you give a fuck about yourself BUT you're also too tired to do anything more than the absolute minimum. This is your new minimum—fucking embrace it.

About 6 cups of mixed lettuces, like romaine, red leaf, and butter (or your favorites)

3 to 4 tablespoons House Vinaigrette (recipe follows)

Salt and black pepper

¼ cup chopped fresh herbs, such as dill, basil, chives, or parsley

Throw your lettuce in a big bowl, drizzle with a little dressing, and add a pinch each of salt and pepper. Toss until everything looks coated, then add the fresh herbs and toss again. Taste and add more dressing or whatever you think it needs. It's always better to add more dressing at the end than too much at the beginning because you can't remove that shit.

House Vinaigrette

Makes about 1 cup / Cook time: 5 minutes

1 shallot or ¼ white or red onion, minced

½ teaspoon garlic powder

¼ teaspoon black pepper

1 tablespoon ume plum vinegar

Juice of 1 lemon (about 2 tablespoons)

¼ cup rice vinegar

¼ cup red wine vinegar or sherry vinegar

¼ cup olive oil

In a small jar with a lid, throw everything together and shake the shit out of it until it looks all incorporated. Have a busy week ahead but want time for salads? Triple this batch and store it in the jar you used to shake it all up. The ingredients will separate as it sits because you don't have a bunch of bullshit stabilizers and gelling agents in there. Don't freak. Just shake it again before you pour. This should keep for at least 10 days in the fridge. If your fridge is super cold, the oil could solidify. If that happens, just place the dressing container under some warm water or leave it on the counter for a bit to warm and loosen up before shaking.

CHEAT SHEET:

Accidently add too much dressing? Don't live that life. Add more lettuce until it looks right and get ready to eat more salad than planned. Overdressed salad is fucking gross, so fix it before it ruins your relationship with lettuce.

FIELD GUIDE:
GARDEN SALAD MANIFESTO

Salads have gotten a bad reputation thanks to terrible cooks and lazy restaurants. Trust us when we say that a few simple tricks can turn this boring plate filler into a craveable meal component that's essential to every meal.

LET'S TALK GREENS

Choosing the right lettuce for the job is crucial to reach salad success. The lettuce should make up about 60 to 70 percent of your finished salad, so if you pick a leaf that can't hang with the rest of your ingredients, then the whole thing is destined to suck. Think of this like picking the noodles for a pasta dish. The shape, taste, and texture of the pasta lends itself better to some styles of sauce than others. It's the same with lettuce. Crispy romaine can hold up to your heavier dressings like our Dill Buttermilk Dressing (page 89), while butter lettuce's soft leaves pair better with a light vinaigrette like our House Vinaigrette (page 51). Once you start thinking about it, the rest is intuitive. Light leaf = lighter dressing.

Washing your lettuce is the next step to salad success for two reasons. One, your lettuce is dirty as fuck even if the bag swears it's triple-washed. Secondly, lettuce is a plant, so it starts drying out the moment it's picked, just like flowers do. Giving the leaves a good bath helps crisp 'em back up. We like to lightly rinse, chop, then do a thorough wash. Run the heads of lettuce under cool water or fill up a bowl and give them a dunk, making sure all the grit and gunk sinks to the bottom. This is just enough of a wash to keep your cutting board clean while you cut that fucker up. You aren't putting dirty vegetables on your cutting board before you wash them, right? RIGHT?

After you cut up your lettuce, give the leaves a good second wash, but don't just throw them back in the bowl when you're done. Not drying your lettuce off before you make a salad is a weirdly common mistake that fucks up the whole bowl. The water that is still on the leaves mixes with the dressing and waters the whole thing down. It's gross. We don't believe in buying tons of kitchen gadgets, but if you're gonna be serious about salads, you'll want a salad spinner. They're affordable, last forever, and double as lettuce storage devices. The centrifugal force of the spinner shoots all the water off the leaves, out the slotted sides of the cage in the center, and it pools in the bottom of the spinner where you can pour it out. Then store whatever lettuce you don't use in there. The cage allows for lots of airflow, guaranteeing your lettuce will stay fresher longer than if it was sitting in a pool of water stuffed in a plastic bag. Ours basically lives in the fridge. A watery salad doesn't deserve a place on your plate.

5-15%
TOPPERS

25%
ADD-INS

60-70%
LETTUCE

FRIENDLY REMINDER TO
EAT A FUCKING SALAD

BUILD THAT BOWL

If you're just making a side salad, lettuce and a few herbs are the way to go. But if you want to make something to upstage your entrée, you're gonna need to put in a little more work. What you add to your lettuce will determine all kinds of things on your road to salad satisfaction: nutrient density, texture, aesthetic appeal, and how full you feel and for how long. To make this more manageable we've broken this idea down into two categories: the add-ins and the toppers.

THE ADD-INS: These are all the additional ingredients you incorporate into the body of the salad and should account for about 25 percent of the whole dish. Here is where you add chopped-up vegetables and fruits like carrots, cucumbers, bell peppers, beets, tomatoes, apples, and whatever the hell you like or is in season. Fuck it, add leftover roasted veggies while you're at it. Leftover cooked grains and beans are great here, too. All these lil' extras bring a fistful of vitamins and minerals to your dish while adding even more heart-healthy, belly-filling fiber.

Once you're done chopping all your add-ins, you can lightly season them right on your cutting board. Just sprinkle a little salt right on top, maybe a squeeze of lemon, or a dash of garlic powder. Treat them with some fucking respect and season them like you would when making any other kind of meal. Bland salads aren't tolerated around here. SEASON ALL THE PARTS.

THE TOPPERS: These are the kind of things that usually draw you to a particular salad in the first place, like croutons, pita chips, or candied nuts. These comprise one of the smallest percentages of your salad but bring a huge amount of the flavor. You aren't trying to be virtuous here. Just add what makes you fucking happy to eat, like toasted nuts, olives, our Crispy Rice Bits (page 74), chopped fresh herbs like dill, sprouts, raw onions, or a handful of croutons (see Onion Croutons, page 58). This 5 to 15 percent of your salad is like the bow on your nutritionally dense gift of a meal.

We like to dress and toss our salads full of all the add-ins, and then add the toppers and toss gently one more time. That way the toppers stay kinda prominent and don't get soggy if they are meant to be crispy. If you're dishing up the salads, save some toppers on the side to sprinkle over the top of each serving when plating for *vibe* reasons.

Now all you need to do is dress that shit. We've got plenty of great options in here but when in doubt, always reach for our updated House Vinaigrette (page 51). It's easy to make, and no one will be able to figure out exactly why it's so delicious. Healthy and mysterious? Fuck yes.

Makes about 1 cup dressing, enough for about 4 side salads /
Cook time: 15 minutes

California Garden Dressing and Side Salad

This salad features our updated take on the classic hippie green goddess dressing. Tarragon is the herb doing the heavy lifting here, but if you can't find it, it's still damn delicious. Don't forget to think outside of the confines of salad and use this dressing as a dip or sandwich spread. Try it pretty much anywhere you'd wanna put an avocado.

Dressing

1 large avocado, halved and pitted

1 shallot, chopped, or ¼ cup chopped onion

Juice of 1 lemon (about 2 tablespoons)

3 tablespoons white wine vinegar

2 tablespoons rice vinegar

2 tablespoons water

2 tablespoons each chopped fresh chives, parsley, and tarragon, or some combo of your faves

¼ teaspoon salt

Salad

Your favorite lettuce, washed and chopped, about 6 cups

Black pepper

Chopped herbs (left over from the dressing)

1 Make the dressing: Scoop the avocado into your food processor or blender along with the shallot, lemon juice, both vinegars, the water, herbs, and salt. Run until smooth because people are rarely down with a chunky-as-fuck salad dressing. The dressing is best the day it's made, but it will last 3 days in the fridge before the avocado starts to brown and betray you.

2 For the salad, toss the dressing with your favorite chopped lettuce and a little black pepper. Top with whatever chopped herbs you have left over.

CHEAT SHEET:

The dressing makes a great and unexpected spread for a sandwich or wrap. Try it on our Broiled Tomato Sandwiches (page 60) instead of the hummus or as a dip at your next party with some Herbed Flatbreads (page 128) cut into strips.

Onion Croutons

Croutons are a welcome addition to any meal, but do you know what makes them even better? Crispy, roasted bits of onion. Make these extra-delicious crunchy sons of bitches and wonder why you never thought of this before. We love them tossed in our West Coast Chopped Salad (page 71), on top of our White Mac and Cheese (page 177), or floating in our Farro and Red Bean Soup (page 120). Hell, just keep them in a jar and snack as needed. No judgment here.

½ **loaf day-old bread**

3 tablespoons olive or avocado oil

½ **yellow onion, minced**

1½ **tablespoons fresh lemon juice**

1½ **teaspoons garlic powder**

¼ **teaspoon paprika**

¼ **teaspoon salt**

1 Warm the oven up to 400°F.

2 Tear your bread into bite-size pieces with your hands. You should get around 5 cups. In a big bowl, combine the oil, onion, lemon juice, garlic powder, paprika, and salt and toss everything together until the onion looks well coated. Add the bread and mix that fucker up to make sure all those pieces get some love, too.

3 Pour that mixture out evenly onto a baking sheet and bake for 20 minutes, stirring it halfway through to make sure that everything gets evenly toasted.

4 Serve right away. You can also keep them in an airtight container for up to 5 days, but we'd love to see you make it that long.

Hippie Hummus Wraps

Every hippie café since the '70s has had this on their menu FOR A GOOD FUCKING REASON. It's delicious. These wraps make a quick and surprisingly satisfying lunch or dinner when you want something fresh but more filling than a salad. Plus, you don't have to turn the stove on at all. Let's keep it on the menu at your place.

½ batch 5-Minute Hummus (page 92)

4 large tortillas or some Herbed Flatbreads (page 128)

1 cucumber, cut into matchsticks

1 tomato, chopped

¼ red or white onion, thinly sliced

1 romaine heart, sliced into ribbons, or our Everyday Cabbage Slaw (page 67)

1 cup clover or alfalfa sprouts (optional)

½ cup chopped fresh herbs, such as basil, cilantro, dill, mint, parsley, and/or cilantro

Lemon halves

Salt and black pepper

1 We know this isn't rocket science, but the only thing you need to keep in mind while you're making these is to not overfill them so you can actually wrap these fuckers up. Michelle's eyes are always bigger than her stomach, so this shit continues to be an issue. Be better than us, k?

2 To make a wrap, spread a couple spoonfuls of hummus down the middle of your tortilla, leaving an inch or two on either end. Throw the cucumbers, tomato, onion, and lettuce down the side of the hummus pile. On top of the hummus, add some sprouts (if using) and a couple tablespoons of the fresh herbs. Squeeze a little lemon juice over the whole thing and sprinkle on salt and pepper. Now wrap that shit up (if you can) and enjoy.

CHEAT SHEET:

Wanna take this to-go but don't want to eat a soggy lunch? Pack all the veggies on top of the hummus in one container and the tortilla in another. Plop everything on the tortilla when it's time to grub and no one, particularly your mouth, will know the difference.

Broiled Tomato Sandwiches

This is an upgrade from the standard tomato sandwich beloved by cool grandpas and Harriet the Spy. It's your new quintessential summer sammie, and it'll be ready in less than 20 minutes.

1 large tomato

¼ teaspoon salt

¼ teaspoon black pepper

1 tablespoon red wine vinegar

1 tablespoon balsamic vinegar

Bread Crumb Coating

1 cup almond milk

1 cup panko bread crumbs

½ cup corn flour, finely ground cornmeal, or masa harina

2 tablespoon nutritional yeast (nooch)

1 teaspoon garlic powder

¼ teaspoon salt

Spray olive oil

Sandwiches

4 slices bread, toasted

Hummus or mayo

Cucumber slices

Basil leaves

Red onion strips

1 Slice your tomato into rounds no thicker than ¼ inch. You should get enough slices for two sammies. Sprinkle them with the salt and pepper and drizzle both vinegars over them. We're building flavor, y'all.

2 Make the bread crumb coating: Pour the milk in a shallow bowl. In another, mix together the bread crumbs, corn flour, nooch, garlic powder, and salt.

3 Turn on the broiler of your oven and let that shit warm up. If your oven has settings for the broiler, high is the way to go.

4 Grab your baking sheet, line it with some parchment paper, and put it near your two-bowl dunking station. Grab a seasoned tomato slice, toss it into the bread crumb mixture, then quickly dunk it in the milk and then back into the bread crumbs for a nice thick crust. Set this on your baking sheet and keep going until you run out of tomato slices. Spray each slice with a little olive oil and stick the baking sheet until the broiler, flipping halfway through, until they are golden brown on both sides, 6 to 10 minutes. The cook time will depend on your broiler, but the golden-brown color will come, trust us.

5 Serve a slice or two of these tomatoes warm between 2 slices of toasted bread with hummus or mayo, sliced cucumbers, some basil leaves, and strips of red onion.

Spicy Peanut and Cilantro Salad

This salad is very loosely inspired by a side at one of our favorite restaurants in LA, Pine and Crane. If you ever have the chance to visit, you must go and eat there. For the rest of you, we have this surprisingly delightful salad made of stuff you might never think to throw together on your own. We love it as a snack or as part of a large spread alongside our Coconut Rice (page 112) or Sesame Noodles with Pan-Seared Tofu (page 154). Hell, we've even been known to put the leftovers on top of some Breakfast Fried Rice (page 22).

2 cups raw peanuts

1 teaspoon soy sauce or tamari

2 teaspoons rice vinegar

1 Fresno chile or jalapeño, seeded and minced

1 shallot or ¼ red onion, minced

½ cup sliced green onions

1 cup packed chopped fresh cilantro

2 teaspoons toasted sesame oil

Juice of ½ lime (about 1 tablespoon)

Salt

Grab a large skillet and warm it up over medium heat. Add the peanuts and dry-sauté them until they start to get a little toasty, about 5 minutes. Remove from the heat and drizzle in the soy sauce and rice vinegar. Toss the peanuts around so they all get coated. Dump the peanuts into a medium bowl, add the Fresno chile, shallot, green onions, and cilantro, and toss until everything is mixed up. Drizzle with the toasted sesame oil and lime juice, toss again, and taste. Add some salt or whatever you think it needs and serve right away.

Sweet and Salty Cucumber and Carrot Salad

This salad is great when you need to get hydrated AND eat at the same time. We crave it any time the temperature goes over 90 and we lose our appetite for anything that isn't refreshing as fuck. Eat it as is or folded into our Pan-Seared Tofu Banh Mi–Inspired Sammie (page 64).

5 Persian (mini) cucumbers, cut lengthwise into thin spears, then cut crosswise into 2-inch-long pieces

Pinch of salt

Dressing

¼ cup rice vinegar

2 tablespoons soy sauce or tamari

1 teaspoon agave or maple syrup

1 garlic clove, minced

1 teaspoon minced fresh ginger

Salad

2 carrots, shredded on a box grater

¼ red onion, sliced into thin strips

¼ cup sliced green onions

2 tablespoons toasted sesame seeds

1 In a medium bowl, toss the cucumbers together with the salt. Let them sit while you chop up everything else.

2 Make the dressing: In a small glass, whisk together the vinegar, soy sauce, agave, garlic, and ginger.

3 Make the salad: Drain away any water that came out of the cucumbers while they were sitting, then toss the carrots and red onion together with them. Drizzle with the dressing you just made and toss again. Sprinkle in the sliced green onions and sesame seeds, then serve right away or let it chill in the fridge for a bit. Any longer than a couple hours and the cucumbers will lose their crispiness, so make it the same day you plan on eating it.

Makes 4 sandwiches / Cook time: 45 minutes, mostly inactive

Pan-Seared Tofu Banh Mi-Inspired Sammie

There's nothing traditional about this banh mi, but damn if it isn't delicious. Try to find a good baguette that's crispy on the outside but airy and light on the inside; otherwise, biting through this beast of a sammie might be fucking difficult. Not a fan of tofu? Make something else. This isn't for you unless you're willing to change.

Pan-Seared Tofu

1 package (14 ounces) extra-firm tofu, drained

¼ cup soy sauce or tamari

2 tablespoons rice vinegar

1 tablespoon hot sauce, like chili-garlic sauce or Sriracha

1 tablespoon fresh lime juice

2 teaspoons toasted sesame oil

2 teaspoons agave or maple syrup

1 teaspoon Chinese 5-spice powder (optional)

1 tablespoon plain, unroasted peanut oil

Sandwiches

2 French baguettes

Sriracha Aioli (see Tofu Mayo Cheat Sheet, page 95)

Chopped fresh cilantro, mint, and basil

Sliced fresh jalapeños

Sweet and Salty Cucumber and Carrot Salad (page 63) or thinly sliced cucumbers tossed in some rice vinegar

1 Prepare the tofu: Wrap the tofu in a clean towel or some paper towels and set something heavy, like a heavy pan, on top to wick away the moisture. Let it get squashed there for at least 15 minutes and up to 45 minutes. Do whatever you've got time for, but don't sweat if you're short on time—longer than 15 isn't better necessarily.

2 While the tofu is pressing, make the marinade: In a small glass, mix the soy sauce, rice vinegar, hot sauce, lime juice, sesame oil, agave, and 5-spice powder (if using).

3 When the tofu is ready, tear it into bite-size cubes with your hands, place them in a bowl, and pour in the marinade. Let this sit, mixing them around occasionally, for at least 15 minutes and up to 2 hours.

4 When you are ready to get this shit going, heat up a large skillet over medium heat with the peanut oil. Reserving a couple tablespoons of the marinade, drain the tofu and toss it around in the pan until all the pieces have a little oil on them. The oil might splatter a bit since the tofu is juicy, so watch the fuck out and turn down the heat if the pan is spitting back at you too much.

5 Cook the pieces on as many sides as possible until light golden brown. This should take 5 to 7 minutes. You aren't gonna get it all even, so don't even try. Some burned parts are IDEAL. Tofu that's a little burned is delicious, so you aren't fucking up at all. When all of the tofu is at least golden in several spots, pour the reserved marinade over them and stir it up. This should evaporate quickly, leaving the tofu looking nice and glossy. Remove from the heat.

6 To make the sandwiches, cut the baguettes in half crosswise, then slice into them from the side without cutting all the way through. Your baguettes will have a little Pac-Man mouth for the sandwich fixings. Slather in some of the Sriracha aioli, and add some fresh herbs, the jalapeños, and a handful of the cucumber and carrot salad (or sliced cucumbers in rice vinegar). Top with the pan-seared tofu and some more herbs, and eat right away.

FIELD GUIDE:
TEARING TOFU

We've been eating tofu for decades and preparing it just how we were taught: cutting it into little cubes or triangles. But recently, we were converted to hand-torn tofu and we're never going back. Tearing the tofu into bite-size pieces with your hands after pressing it not only makes the protein look more delicious, but all those nooks and crannies you create help the marinade get even deeper into the tofu, making it extra flavorful.

Below is our pan-seared tofu (see Pan-Seared Tofu Banh Mi-Inspired Sammie, page 64). We cut the tofu on the right side of the plate into cubes and tore the tofu on the left by hand. Look how good that torn tofu looks compared to the cubes. Lesson over.

CUBED TOFU

HAND-TORN TOFU

Everyday Cabbage Slaw

Are you the kind of person who can't use all the lettuce in your crisper before that shit turns into mush? This is the salad for you. Cabbage keeps WAAYYY longer in the fridge and you can always halve this recipe if you're just trying to make sure you get some greens in even when you're cooking for one. We love this alongside our El Congrí de Flor (page 172) or in our Hippie Hummus Wraps (page 59).

½ **head green cabbage, thinly sliced**

¼ **teaspoon salt**

2 tablespoons fresh lime juice

1 tablespoon rice vinegar

1 tablespoon olive oil

1 teaspoon ume plum vinegar (optional)

2 tablespoons minced green onions, chives, or cilantro

In a large bowl, place the shredded cabbage and sprinkle with the salt. With your hands, get in there and kinda smoosh up the cabbage with the salt. This will help break down the cabbage, so it doesn't taste like you are eating an oppressive amount of fiber. Trust us. Drizzle with the lime juice, rice vinegar, olive oil, and plum vinegar. No plum vinegar? Just taste and see if it needs more salt. Now stir in the herbs you minced and serve right away. Easy as hell.

CHEAT SHEET:

Wanna mix it up? Change the herbs based on what you're serving with this slaw. Add a grated garlic clove, thinly sliced onion, carrots, or even cucumber. Switch out the lime juice for lemon and the olive oil for toasted sesame oil. Throw in some celery, sesame seeds, or poppy seeds. Basically, there are endless ways to customize this slaw to fit whatever the fuck you pair it with.

Grilled Romaine and Carrot Salad with Dill Buttermilk Dressing

Any motherfucker can grill a burger or hot dog. Real motherfuckers can grill anything, like a salad. Hell, even Gordon Ramsay has come around to grilled lettuce, so you should, too. Grab those tongs and click-clack your grill skills up a notch.

2 garlic cloves, minced

¼ cup olive oil

Salt and black pepper

3 to 4 romaine hearts or baby romaine heads, cleaned and halved lengthwise

Dill Buttermilk Dressing (page 89)

1 carrot

1 cucumber, chopped

¼ red onion, thinly sliced

Chopped herbs (left over from the dressing)

1 Heat the grill or a stovetop grill pan to medium heat.

2 While the grill heats up, mix the garlic, olive oil, and a pinch each of salt and pepper in a little cup. Brush or spoon the oil mixture on the cut side of the lettuce. This isn't the fucking dressing, so go easy.

3 Place the lettuce cut side down on the hot grill for 60 seconds or until there are clear grill marks and the leaves start to wilt. Flip the hearts over and grill the other side for another 60 seconds. You want the leaves to look charred but not limp, SO PAY FUCKING ATTENTION. When they look good, put 'em on a plate and let 'em cool for a minute.

4 When you're ready to serve those charred motherfuckers, drizzle some dressing on a large plate or sheet pan and place the grilled romaine hearts on there. Then, grab the carrot and shave thin strips over the lettuce using a veggie peeler. Toss on the cucumber and red onion, drizzle some dressing over the hearts, and top with some of the herbs left over from making the dressing, then crack over some more pepper. Serve right away.

West Coast Chopped Salad

Chopped salad can be made from almost anything if you chop the components about the same size, but this one is our favorite. It's a showstopper at any summer dinner party and takes hardly any time to throw together. Half the fun of a chopped salad is its composed presentation. (See what we did there in the photo?) Taking the time to go for the prettiest presentation will make the resulting dish taste that much better, even if you're just making it for yourself. You deserve cute shit. The other half of the fun of a chopped salad? Eating it with a fucking spoon.

2 romaine hearts, cleaned and chopped into ribbons no thicker than ½ inch

1½ cups sliced cherry or grape tomatoes

2 Persian cucumbers or ½ English cucumber, chopped into cubes about the size of dice

1 cup grilled corn kernels, from 2 grilled cobs (see Corn, page 227), or defrosted frozen kernels

2 grilled zucchinis, chopped into cubes (see Summer Squash, page 228)

1 cup chopped red onion

½ cup roughly chopped cilantro

1 avocado, sliced

Salt and black pepper

Cashew Buttermilk Dressing (page 88) or House Vinaigrette (page 51)

Grab a large bowl and throw in the romaine hearts. Start piling ingredients on top of the romaine in their own sections with the avocado in the center. Just make it pretty, okay? Top everything with a little salt and pepper to taste and drizzle your choice of dressing over the bowl. To serve, bring the salad to the table like this, then just toss everything together before everyone digs in.

Makes 6 wedges, enough for 1 to 6 people, depending on how much everyone likes salad / Cook time: 30 minutes

BLT Wedge Salads

Wedge salads are a great gateway into the Salad Lifestyle™. They're gorgeous, fun to eat, and make salads seem like an event rather than a dish to survive at dinnertime. The B in our BLT stands for "bits," as in Crispy Rice Bits. We like to dress these wedges on individual salad plates for a fancy dinner. Otherwise, just make them all on a sheet pan and set them out with tongs for serving. Either way, the people will love it.

Cashew Buttermilk Dressing (page 88)

1 tablespoon hemp seeds (optional)

1 head iceberg lettuce, cut into 6 wedges

2 cups sliced cherry tomatoes

½ cup minced red onion

¼ cup minced chives

Crispy Rice Bits (recipe follows)

Black pepper

1 Make the dressing as directed and if you want, just for looks, fold in the hemp seeds.

2 You probably have the gist on how to assemble this just from looking at the picture, but here it goes anyway. Put the lettuce wedge on a plate, then drizzle the dressing over it. Use that shit like glue to get the toppings to stick. Sprinkle with the tomatoes, red onion, and the minced chives. Drizzle with a little more dressing and top with the crispy rice bits and finish with some fresh cracked black pepper.

3 This salad will look almost too beautiful to eat, but you're def gonna want to eat it. Serve each wedge with a fork and knife so people can cut it up and dig in.

(recipe continues)

Crispy Rice Bits

Makes a little over 1 cup / Cook time: 15 minutes

2 teaspoons Bragg Liquid Aminos

1 teaspoon rice vinegar

1 teaspoon liquid smoke

1 teaspoon maple syrup

½ teaspoon garlic powder

1 tablespoon olive oil

1 cup cold cooked plain rice

1 Mix together the liquid aminos, rice vinegar, liquid smoke, maple syrup, and garlic powder together in a small glass. Set that aside—we're coming back to it.

2 Warm up a large sauté pan or skillet over medium-high heat and add the oil. Crumble the cold rice into the pot and sauté it around until it's all coated in oil. Keep sautéing it around for a couple minutes until the rice warms up. If you are having a hard time, add a tablespoon or two of water to the pan to help get the rice moving. Once the rice is warm, pile it in the center of the pan and drizzle the sauce mixture from step 1 over the top and stir it around so that all the rice gets coated.

3 Spread the rice into as thin a layer as possible in the pan. Stir it around every now and then, but the point is to get the rice as crispy as possible, 5 to 7 minutes. Press it down against the heat of the pan with the back of your spoon as you cook it to speed up the process. You'll know it's ready when all the liquid is gone from the pan and the rice is crispy. Place it on a dry paper towel. Serve right away or store it in an airtight jar in the fridge for up to 1 week.

King Club Sammies

Yeah, it looks like there are a lot of steps to make a sandwich, but it comes together way faster than you think. You're right to be skeptical of the tofu in here, but hot damn, does it really add something to the overall sandwich experience. We wouldn't throw it in there for no reason. The king trumpet mushroom bacon strips bring a shit-ton of umami and smoky flavor to the mix making each bite a fucking taste explosion. Just trust us on this and make time for this sammie.

1 tablespoon avocado or olive oil

1 package (14 ounces) extra-firm tofu, drained

Salt

1 tablespoon no-salt, all-purpose seasoning (your favorite)

½ cup vegetable broth

1 tablespoon nutritional yeast (nooch)

½ teaspoon garlic powder

Black pepper

King Trumpet Mushroom Bacon Strips

¼ cup vegetable broth

1 tablespoon Bragg Liquid Aminos or soy sauce

1 tablespoon ume plum vinegar or more liquid aminos

2 teaspoons maple syrup

1 teaspoon tomato paste

1 teaspoon liquid smoke

1 tablespoon avocado or olive oil

1 First, let's make the protein of the sandwich. In a large sauté pan with a lid, warm up the avocado oil over medium-high heat. Slice the brick of tofu into wide slabs about ¼ inch thick so you end up with around 4 sliced pieces that have the same surface area as the top of the tofu. Swirl the oil around in the hot pan to make sure you've got a thin layer over the entire surface, then place the tofu and kinda press it into the pan. Sprinkle the top with a pinch of salt and half of the all-purpose seasoning. Sear the tofu until the bottom looks toasted in some spots, about 3 minutes, pressing down on each slab with the back of the spatula. You should hear it hiss. Flip and repeat the process.

2 Once both sides are looking golden brown, add the vegetable broth and throw on the lid. Let this cook for 4 minutes, just long enough for the tofu to get the chance to absorb a lot of the flavor. Uncover, flip the tofu again, and sprinkle with the rest of the all-purpose seasoning, nooch, garlic powder, and black pepper. Keep cooking until all the liquid has left the pot. Place the tofu on a plate.

(recipe and ingredients continue)

CHEAT SHEET:

Serve with a Simple Side Salad with House
Vinaigrette (page 51), Everyday Cabbage Slaw
(page 67), Sunshine Pasta Salad (page 126),
or with some chips and a pickle.

4 large king trumpet mushrooms,* cut lengthwise into thin slices

Sandwiches

8 slices bread, toasted

Tofu Mayo (page 95)

Mustard

Avocado, sliced

Tomato, sliced

Lettuce

*King trumpet mushrooms, sometimes called king oysters or French horn mushrooms, are known for their thick but tender stems and relatively small caps. This makes them the perfect mushroom to cut into thin bacon-shaped strips. If you can't find them, 2 large portobellos will work in a pinch.

3 Make the mushroom bacon strips: In a small glass, mix together the broth, liquid aminos, ume plum vinegar, maple syrup, tomato paste, and liquid smoke. Set the pan you were just using for the tofu back over the heat and add the oil to it. Toss in the mushroom slices and sauté them around until they start softening up and releasing some of their moisture, 3 to 4 minutes.

4 Pour in the broth mixture and stir to make sure the mushrooms get covered. Let this cook, stirring often, until the liquid has left the pan, 3 to 5 minutes. If you want this bacon crispy, throw it under your broiler for 3 to 4 additional minutes to crisp up. It's good either way.

5 Assemble the sandwiches: Spread 1 slice of toast with some tofu mayo and spread mustard on a second slice. Press avocado into the slice with the mustard. Layer tomato slices on the side with the mayo, then add one slab of the tofu. Place lettuce on top of the tofu, then the mushroom bacon. Now smash that avocado side right down on the bacon, and boom, you've got a sandwich.

FIELD GUIDE:
HOW TO STACK A SANDWICH

After much trial and error, we have arrived at the optimal method for stacking a sandwich. If you follow this approach, you'll have years of delicious meals ahead of you instead of whatever dark path you're currently on. Trust us: Life is better with a well-built sammie.

FIRST you want bread that has been toasted golden brown on one side, and very, very lightly toasted on the other. The darker side faces out and the lighter side goes inside the sammie to better hold the ingredients and absorb the flavors. Bread that is overly toasted on both sides leads to sammie instability, which we must avoid.

NEXT goes your sauce or condiment of choice, right onto the top slice of bread. This is also a great layer to add your avocado, nondairy cheese, or anything fatty and soft. Having the soft stuff like this up top allows you to bite through the sammie easily instead of having to gnaw through something hard and fuck up the whole sandwich.

THEN comes your crispy crunch layer. This is where you put your lettuce, chips, or our trumpet mushroom bacon (see King Club Sammies, page 75). Pickle slices or sliced onion are great, too. A crunch layer is a must, but don't go too crazy. Too much shit in your crunch layer, and it'll all fall out of the back of the sammie as soon as you bite into it.

NEXT, it's time for the protein or the main flavor component. This could be the tofu in our King Club Sammies (page 75), the blender egg in our Blender Breakfast Sammies (page 23), or a big Quinoa Zucchini Fritter (page 142). By placing the heart of the sandwich here, it gets all the flavor from the other layers around it. Plus, there's little risk of the sammie falling apart because your sammie star needs to balance on top of a random pile of lettuce. You want this layer nice and cozy.

FINALLY, the last layer is the tomato, with your condiment of choice spread on the bottom slice of bread. The tomato is soft enough to hold up the whole sammie without being hard as fuck to bite through. If you put anything hard or crunchy at the bottom, you're gonna struggle to hold that shit together come lunchtime. Trust us.

Follow this formula, and you'll have yourself a sammie with minimal mess.

BUILD-A-SAMMIE

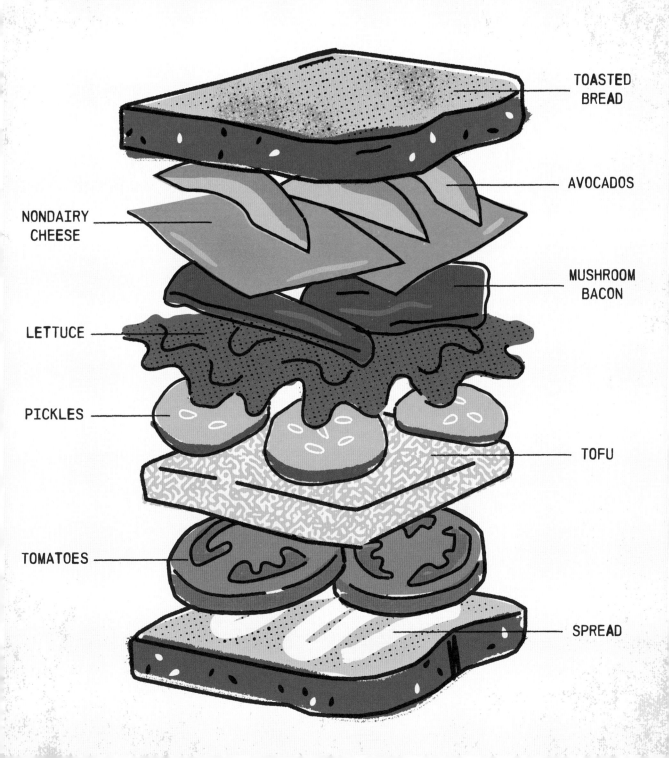

Pepper Cheese Hoagies

This sandwich is the result of some late-night fever dreams involving Philadelphia. It's a gooey mess, but that's part of its charm. Maybe one day we'll make it to Philly. Until then, we'll be eating these in the city's honor.

½ cup vegetable broth

1 tablespoon Bragg Liquid Aminos or soy sauce

1 tablespoon tomato paste

1 tablespoon olive oil

1 yellow or white onion, thinly sliced

2 red and/or green bell peppers, thinly sliced

Salt

1 can (20 ounces) water-packed young jackfruit, drained, rinsed, and chopped*

4 garlic cloves, minced

1 tablespoon no-salt, all-purpose seasoning (your favorite)

1½ cups Queso Blanco (page 96)

Black pepper

4 large hoagie rolls, toasted

*Don't know shit about jackfruit? Learn how to buy and prep it the Field Guide on page 81.

1 In a small glass, mix the broth, liquid aminos, and tomato paste. Set this mixture aside.

2 In your largest sauté pan or skillet, warm up the olive oil over medium-high heat. Add the onion, bell peppers, and a pinch of salt and cook until the onion starts to brown and the peppers soften, about 8 minutes. Add the jackfruit and cook for another 3 minutes, making sure to mix it all in with the onions and peppers. Add the garlic to pan and cook for a minute more.

3 Pour the broth mixture into the pan. Cook, stirring frequently, until most of the marinade has evaporated, 4 to 5 minutes. Add the all-purpose seasoning and cook for another 2 minutes so that all the flavors have time to mix together. Remove from the heat and add 1 cup of the queso and some black pepper. Taste and add more of whatever you think it needs.

4 To serve, scoop the filling into the toasted hoagie rolls and drizzle with the remaining ½ cup queso. Serve warm.

FIELD GUIDE:
HOW TO PREP JACKFRUIT

Fifteen years ago, most people in North America had never heard of jackfruit, and now it's on menus all over and in national grocery chains. It's a tropical fruit, but you won't find this giant motherfucker in the produce section at most stores. It's way more common to find unripe jackfruit in a can rather than fresh. But if you can find one that's fresh, it's something to fucking see. It's MASSIVE.

Jackfruit is the largest fruit on Earth to come from a tree, and it does not disappoint. They can be 3 feet long and 2 feet wide and weigh up to 120 pounds, although 10 to 50 pounds is the average.

As jackfruit ripens, it gets softer and sweeter, tasting almost like a banana or mango. Unripe, it has hardly any taste, which makes it fucking perfect to cook with. It takes on the flavor of whatever you put it in and has a texture similar to pulled pork. When you're grabbing some from the store for any of our recipes, make sure you get unripe or young jackfruit canned in water, not syrup. That sweet shit is good, but not for what we're doing in here.

Now that you've brought your cans of jackfruit home, drain them in a colander and rinse them with cool water. We used to sit there and shred this shit by hand, but we've figured out a much faster way to get this shit ready to cook. Place the rinsed jackfruit on your cutting board and with the broad side of your knife, press down on the chunks of jackfruit to split them apart. Then roughly chop the pieces and remove any of the hard seeds you see. Now your jackfruit is ready for whatever recipe you've lined up, and we've saved you at least 30 minutes of your life. You're welcome.

THAT'S ONE BIG-ASS JACKFRUIT.

Grain Salad with Pecans and Tarragon

Tarragon is one of those fancy-sounding herbs that neither of us grew up eating. Same with farro. But we're intimidated no longer. If farro is new to you too, check out our grain guide on page 219 to learn all about it before you make this dish. This salad is hearty enough to stand on its own against fall and winter entrées, but the tarragon and arugula keep it tasting fresh and light. It's perfect on its own, with a side of our 5-Minute Hummus (page 92), or as part of your Thanksgiving spread.

4 tablespoons olive oil

1 cup farro

1 cup wild rice

Salt

3¾ cups vegetable broth or water

¼ cup sherry vinegar

1 tablespoon ume plum vinegar

1 tablespoon rice vinegar

2 shallots or ½ small red onion, minced

2 cups chopped arugula

½ cup dried cranberries

½ cup chopped pecans or walnuts

¼ cup chopped fresh parsley

1 tablespoon chopped fresh tarragon

Black pepper

1 In a medium to large pot with a lid, warm up 1 tablespoon of the olive oil over medium heat. Add the farro and wild rice and a pinch of salt and stir everything up. Pour in the broth and bring that to a simmer. Once simmering, reduce the heat to low, throw on the lid, and cook until the grains are tender and the liquid is basically gone, 30 to 40 minutes. Once the grains are done, drain away any remaining water and set them in a large bowl to cool.

2 In a small glass, whisk together the remaining 3 tablespoons olive oil, sherry vinegar, plum vinegar, and rice vinegar. When the grains feel about room temperature, drizzle with this dressing and then fold in the shallots, arugula, cranberries, pecans, parsley, and tarragon. Taste and add more salt or pepper or whatever you think it needs. Serve right away.

BBQ Mango Jackfruit Sammies

BBQ and mangoes were meant to be together. Their sticky sweetness goes so perfectly with each other that we don't know why we don't see this shit on every menu. Sure, you could use store-bought BBQ sauce instead, but making your own only takes a couple of minutes. Try it at least once. You deserve something nice.

1½ cups BBQ Mango Sauce (recipe follows)

1½ cups vegetable broth

2 tablespoons Bragg Liquid Aminos or soy sauce

2 tablespoons vegan Worcestershire sauce (or just use more liquid aminos/ soy sauce)

2 tablespoons Tabasco sauce or similar hot sauce

2 teaspoons liquid smoke

3 tablespoons avocado or olive oil

1 large onion, chopped

2 cans (14 ounces each) young jackfruit,* rinsed, drained, and chopped

4 garlic cloves, minced

Spray oil

*Don't know shit about jackfruit? Learn how to buy and prep it in the Field Guide on page 81.

1 In a large measuring cup, mix together the BBQ sauce, broth, liquid aminos, Worcestershire, Tabasco, and liquid smoke. Set the sauce aside.

2 Heat a large ovenproof skillet over medium-high heat. Add the oil and onion and sauté until the onion is golden, about 8 minutes. Add the chopped jackfruit and stir until it begins to stick to the pan, 3 to 5 minutes. Add the garlic and the sauce, stirring to get all the burnt bits off the bottom of the pan. Don't panic. You want those burnt bits. They're flavor, baby.

3 Bring to a simmer, breaking up any large pieces of jackfruit that escaped your knife with a fork or spoon as you stir. Reduce the heat to medium-low and cook, stirring occasionally, until most of the liquid is gone but the jackfruit is still moist, 20 to 25 minutes.

4 When almost all the liquid is gone, remove from the heat and turn your broiler up to high. Spray some oil over the top of the jackfruit and stick it under the broiler for a couple of minutes, until parts start to look a little burnt. Take it out, stir, and repeat the process at least three more times to get some good burnt parts on the jackfruit. This is annoying, but it's totally fucking worth it.

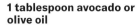

Sammies

4 buns or your favorite bread, split and toasted

Tofu Mayo (page 95)

Everyday Cabbage Slaw (page 67)

Extra BBQ Mango Sauce, for serving

5 For the sammies: Serve the jackfruit on the toasted buns, slathered with tofu mayo and extra BBQ sauce and topped with slaw.

BBQ Mango Sauce

`Makes 3 cups / Cook time: 35 minutes`

1 tablespoon avocado or olive oil

½ red onion, chopped

Salt

2 mangoes, diced, or 2 cups frozen cubed mango

2 garlic cloves, chopped

2 teaspoons smoked paprika

2 chipotle peppers in adobe sauce, seeded and chopped

1 tablespoon Bragg Liquid Aminos

1½ cups or 1 can (15 ounces) tomato sauce

¼ cup packed brown sugar

2 tablespoons apple cider vinegar

1 In a large sauté pan, warm up the olive oil over medium heat. Add the onion with a pinch of salt and sauté until it starts to brown in some spots, about 8 minutes. Add the mango to the pan and cook until the mango starts to really soften up, about another 5 minutes. Add the garlic, smoked paprika, chipotle peppers, and liquid aminos and cook for a minute more until the garlic smells good. Pour in the tomato sauce, brown sugar, and apple cider vinegar. Bring to a simmer, stirring often, until the sugar has dissolved. Simmer for another 5 minutes to really make sure that mango is nice and soft, then remove from the heat.

2 Grab your immersion blender and throw that shit in there. Run until the sauce looks smooth. No immersion blender? Let the sauce cool a little, then dump it into your blender or food processor and run it until smooth. Whatever you use, taste and add more of whatever you think it needs. This will keep for at least a week in the fridge, so feel free to throw it together ahead of time. Leftover sauce is great sautéed with some torn tofu bites (see Field Guide: Tearing Tofu, page 66), or spread on our Pepper Cheese Hoagies (page 80), or as a dip for our Poblano Home Fries (page 38). It's too good to not use every last drop.

Stew
Over

M-F

It

Soups, Sides, and One-Pot Meals

wknd

Makes about 1⅓ cups / Cook time: 15 minutes

Cashew Buttermilk Dressing

This dressing and the dill variation on the opposite page were born out of spite. We love that creamy deliciousness that comes from buttermilk dressings, but since they tend to call for, well, buttermilk and lots of it, that shit just doesn't work for us. Instead, we said fuck that and came up with our own. These double as great dips, hence their presence here in this chapter and not just stuffed next to the salads. They deserve attention all on their own. But if you are looking to make a salad, serve these dressings tossed over some chopped romaine, cucumbers, and tomatoes with some Onion Croutons (page 58).

3 tablespoons cashew butter*

1 shallot or ¼ onion, chopped

Juice of 1 lemon (about 2 tablespoons)

2 tablespoons rice vinegar

1 tablespoon sherry vinegar

1 tablespoon olive oil

1 tablespoon ume plum vinegar

⅓ cup nondairy milk

***Not sure about cashew butter? See our Cheat Sheet on page 97 for an alternative.**

Throw everything in your strongest blender or food processor and run that shit until it looks nice and creamy. Done. You can keep this in the fridge for up to 1 week.

Dill Buttermilk Dressing

Makes about 1½ cups

Cashew Buttermilk Dressing

3 tablespoons chopped fresh dill

2 tablespoons chopped fresh chives

1 teaspoon garlic powder

¼ teaspoon black pepper

1 Make the cashew buttermilk dressing as directed.

2 Once it's all done, add the dill, chives, garlic powder, and black pepper and pulse your blender until everything is all mixed up. Serve right away or chill for bit in the fridge. This is best in the first 3 days of making because after that, the fresh herbs really just quit on you.

CHEAT SHEET:

Want more? You can customize our Cashew Buttermilk Dressing by adding whatever you want to the base. Add garlic and lime juice and pulse until combined. Throw in some cilantro. Switch out the vinegars. Add black pepper, your favorite herbs, and more lemon juice. You make this match your meal however you want. It's always best within the first 3 days of being made, but it will keep for 5 in the fridge at least. If you stick it in the fridge for at least 15 minutes, it'll thicken up and make a dip so luscious that everyone will want the damn recipe. Need some guidance? Here's one of our favorite versions.

FIELD GUIDE:
HOW TO CRUDITÉ

Crudité is just a fancy French way of saying a fresh veggie tray that often comes with a dip. We've all seen horrible examples of this shit at parties where the carrots are dried out, the dip is hot, or all that's left on the tray are the green bell pepper strips and giant chunks of raw broccoli. It doesn't have to be like this. Follow our lead and you'll be able to slap together a crudité platter worthy of center stage on any table, whether it's for a party or just a movie night on the couch when you don't wanna eat a bunch of junk.

First, pick veggies that look fresh and are relatively in season:

- DEAD OF **WINTER**? PASS ON THE CHERRY TOMATOES AND GRAB SOME RAINBOW CARROTS INSTEAD, AS WELL AS BABY LETTUCES, BROCCOLINI, AND CRISP CABBAGE LEAVES.

- **SPRING** HAS SPRUNG? LOOK FOR SUGAR SNAP PEAS, BABY SQUASH, AND SWEET RADISHES.

- **SUMMER** IS GREAT FOR TOMATOES, GREEN BEANS, BABY CORN, AND SWEET PEPPERS.

- **FALL** IS A GOOD TIME TO FEATURE CELERY, ENDIVE, AND SLICES OF CRISP APPLES AND PEARS.

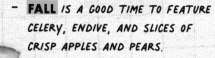

Trust your gut and pick produce that looks appealing to you. Putting out a tray of ugly, wilting, bruised veggies isn't gonna do anybody any favors.

Next, you want to make sure that you're mixing in different textures. If you've got a tray of all crunchy veggies like carrots and celery, your mouth gets kinda bored. It's science. Throw in something soft yet crisp, like cucumber or some blanched broccoli. Sliced grape tomatoes are great, but if you put them out unsliced, you're basically leaving little bombs that may or may not explode all over the place as soon as your guests bite into them. Proceed with caution. Consider throwing some pickled green beans or cauliflower on there. They can be tough and sorta flavorless when raw, but pickled, they're softer and waaay more flavorful.

Plus, a tray of raw cauliflower is just a down payment on farts.

Why do that to people? Bottom line: Adding different kinds of veggies prepared in different ways makes the tray looks nicer because of the variety. The whole dish becomes way more interesting to eat.

Remember that these veggies might need some extra love and seasoning. Once you arrange the veggies on your plate, consider sprinkling on some seasoning. A little fresh lemon juice, a pinch of salt, sumac, or everything bagel seasoning not only makes the arrangement look extra cute, but it also makes that shit even more delicious—which ultimately is the point. If the tray is gonna sit out for a while—like at a party—think about filling a spray bottle with a little water and misting the tray every now and then.

These veggies are like fresh flowers: With no water, they will wilt and get less appealing over time.

A spritz or two of water will wake their asses up and keep them looking fresh.

Finally, choose a dip or dips that complement the whole tray. We love our classic 5-Minute Hummus (page 92), but the Cashew Buttermilk Dressing (page 88) is endlessly customizable and great as a dip. Our Yellow Split Pea Dip (page 118) would be great with the Herbed Flatbreads (page 128) cut into slices for good measure. Happy dipping, motherfuckers!

5-Minute Hummus

Stop buying store hummus and learn to make your own from scratch. It'll taste significantly better than what's sitting on the shelf, and it'll take 5 fucking minutes. You've got 5 minutes and soon you'll have homemade hummus.

3 cups cooked chickpeas, or 2 cans (15 ounces each), drained and rinsed

⅓ cup tahini

¼ cup olive oil

¼ cup fresh lemon juice (about 2 lemons)

½ teaspoon salt or 1 tablespoon ume plum vinegar

½ teaspoon ground cumin

Topping Ideas

Chopped fresh herbs

Dried thyme

Sumac

Paprika

Everything bagel seasoning

Olive oil

1 Throw everything into a blender or food processor and run that shit until it looks smooth. If you need more liquid to get that shit running, add a tablespoon or two of water to the blender at a time until you get the consistency you want. Serve right away or let it chill in the fridge for a while.

2 Top with some fresh or dried herbs, a sprinkle of sumac or paprika or everything bagel seasoning, and a drizzle of olive oil. Store in the fridge, and it will keep for at least a week.

CHEAT SHEET:

This recipe is a great, everyday hummus, but it's also a perfect base for tons of other flavors. Throw in a chipotle pepper in adobo sauce (see WTF Ingredients, page 221) for a spicy smoky flavor, add a roasted bell pepper or garlic to take it in a whole other direction. Drizzle in some pesto or chopped cilantro for an herbaceous take on the classic. Switch out the beans and try it with black-eyed peas or black beans. Basically, if you can think it, you can hummus it.

Tahini Cucumber Sauce

Inspired by tzatziki, this sauce makes a great addition to any crudité spread (see Field Guide, page 90), on top of our Falafel Waffle (page 141), or tossed over cold noodles for a simple pasta salad.

3 tablespoons tahini

Juice of 1 lemon (about 2 tablespoons)

1 tablespoon water

¼ teaspoon garlic powder

Pinch of salt

1 Persian (mini) cucumber, grated like cheese on a box grater (about ½ cup)

Mix the tahini, lemon juice, water, garlic powder, and salt in a small bowl until the sauce looks creamy and emulsified. Fold the cucumber into the sauce and let it sit in the fridge until its ready to serve. The cucumber will release some juice as it sits, which only adds to the deliciousness. You only need to let this chill for about 10 minutes, so don't stress too much. This will keep in the fridge for about 3 days, but after that it just doesn't taste as good.

Garlic-Mint Yogurt

This savory yogurt is a great way to make acidic dishes, like our Baked Butternut Squash with Tomato Lentil Sauce (page 166), taste downright decadent and creamy. Even mint haters will ask for seconds. It's also great alongside pan-fried foods like our Tomato Chickpea Fritters (page 144), Quinoa Zucchini Fritters (page 142), or other crispy, herby entrees like our Falafel Waffle (page 141).

1 cup nondairy yogurt

1 tablespoon fresh lemon juice

2 garlic cloves, grated or finely minced

2 tablespoons minced fresh mint or 2 teaspoons dried mint

Pinch of salt

Mix everything together in a small bowl and let it sit for at least 15 minutes before serving so that the garlic can really work its way into the yogurt. This will keep in the fridge for about 3 days before the mint starts to taste more grassy than delicious.

Tofu Mayo

Sure, there are plenty of great vegan mayos out there, but sometimes you wanna do that shit yourself. Here's how. We've added garlic because why the fuck not, but technically that makes this more of an aioli. Sounds a helluva lot fancier than it is.

1 block (12 ounces) soft silken tofu*

¼ cup neutral cooking oil, such as avocado oil

1 tablespoon fresh lemon juice

1 teaspoon Dijon mustard

1 or 2 garlic cloves, minced

¼ teaspoon salt

*You want the kind of silken tofu that's shelf stable, not the stuff packed in water in the cold case. You'll find it near the soy sauce at most grocery stores.

Throw everything in a blender or food processor and run that shit until it's smooth in there, about 30 seconds. This will keep in the fridge in a jar for about 1 week. If it starts to separate, just throw it back in the blender and run that shit again.

CHEAT SHEET:

To turn this into Sriracha Aioli, add 2 tablespoons Sriracha or a similar style of hot sauce to the blender and run that shit.

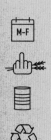

Queso Blanco

This queso is ridiculous. Seriously. Not only is it silky and fucking delicious, it browns in the oven and goes great with our Green Enchiladas (page 171) and inside our Savory Breakfast Hand Pies (page 30). It will solve all the problems in your life, too. Want to make it nut-free? Just add 2 tablespoons of oil to the recipe instead of the cashew butter because nut-free queso is still better than no queso, right?

1 tablespoon olive oil

1 shallot or ¼ onion, chopped

2 russet potatoes, peeled and chopped

1 cup vegetable broth

1 cup nondairy milk

⅓ cup nutritional yeast (nooch)

2 tablespoons cashew butter*

1 tablespoon Bragg Liquid Aminos or tamari

1 tablespoon ume plum vinegar or ½ teaspoon salt

2 tablespoons fresh lemon juice

¼ teaspoon ground cumin

½ cup canned green chiles (optional)

1 jalapeño (optional), minced

*Not sure about cashew butter? See our Cheat Sheet on page 97 for an alternative.

1 In a large sauté pan or skillet with a lid, warm up the olive oil over medium heat. Add the shallot and sauté it around until it gets some color to it, about 5 minutes. Add the chopped potatoes and stir until it's all mixed up with the shallot, then pour in the veggie broth. Cover the pan and let it simmer away until the potatoes are tender enough to easily push a fork through them, about 10 minutes. Let them cool in the pan while you get the rest of the shit ready.

2 In a blender, combine the milk, nooch, cashew butter, liquid aminos, plum vinegar, lemon juice, and cumin. Add the cooled potatoes and whatever broth is still left in the pan to the blender, then let that shit run. To really make a silky queso, you want to run that shit for at least 30 seconds to 1 minute depending on the strength of your blender. Taste it, and if the texture is still a little grainy, keep blending because this shit should be smooth as hell. Once it tastes right, pour it into a large saucepan over low heat. If using the canned chiles and/or the jalapeño, stir them in now. Let the queso warm up. Serve right away.

CHEAT SHEET:

Yeah, we know cashew butter is expensive, but it's the best thing to help this cheese brown when you put it in the oven. To make a cheater version, soak ½ cup cashews in hot water for 30 minutes. Drain off the water and put the cashews in your food processor or blender. Add a little olive or avocado oil so you can get the machine moving. Run it until everything looks nice and smooth and then use that instead of store-bought cashew butter.

Makes 1½ cups / Cook time: 10 minutes

Panko Pasta Topping

Sometimes your pasta needs a little extra crunch or texture to really shine. This easy topping is perfect for such an occasion, but don't limit this shit to just pasta. Sprinkle it on top of roasted veggies like our Sheet Pan Cauliflower with Pumpkin Seeds (page 102), a side salad (see our Simple Side Salad with House Vinaigrette, page 50), or a bowl of soup right before you serve it. We always have a jar on hand and so should you.

3 tablespoons olive oil
1½ cups panko bread crumbs
¼ teaspoon garlic powder
¼ teaspoon paprika
¼ teaspoon salt

In a medium skillet, warm the olive oil over medium-low heat. Add the panko and stir that shit around so everything gets some oil on it. Keep stirring until it starts to look a little golden, 3 to 5 minutes, depending on how low your medium-low heat is. Add the garlic powder, paprika, and salt, and stir until it's all mixed in. Then turn off the heat and pour the topping onto a plate. Use right away or let it cool before storing. This tasty topping will keep for 2 weeks in an airtight container in the fridge.

Grilled Plantains

We love plantains, but we don't love frying them all the damn time. Grilling is a great way to get plantains on the table fast, and they're always a welcome surprise at a BBQ. Seriously, people are always fucking excited to see plantains on the table. We love them alongside our El Congrí de Flor (page 172) and Everyday Cabbage Slaw (page 67), but they're equally killer with our Sunshine Pasta Salad (page 126) or stuffed inside some Savory Breakfast Hand Pies (page 30) with our Cheater Beans (page 138). Our Cilantro Chimichurri (page 100) really takes them to the next level, so if you've got a couple extra minutes, throw that shit together, too.

3 yellow plantains

1 to 2 tablespoons peanut or avocado oil

2 tablespoons fresh lime juice

1 tablespoon brown sugar

Salt

Cilantro Chimichurri (optional; page 100)

1 Heat your grill to medium-high heat.

2 While that's heating up, cut your plantains lengthwise, leaving the peels on. Yeah, we're keeping this shit easy. Brush the cut plantains with the oil on both sides. Place them sliced side down on the grill, close the lid, and cook for 10 minutes.

3 While those are grilling, mix the lime juice and brown sugar in a small glass. After the 10 minutes is up and you've got some good grill marks on the plantains, flip those fuckers over and drizzle on the lime juice mixture. Cover the grill and cook another 10 minutes.

4 When they are all done, cut the long plantains in half crosswise and sprinkle a little salt on top. Serve as is or alongside the cilantro chimichurri.

Makes about 2 cups / Cook time: 5 minutes

Cilantro Chimichurri

Chimichurri is another recipe you should commit to memory because it's so simple and delicious. This herb salsa works as a sauce, a dip, and a late-night confidant. Chimichurri is whatever the fuck you want it to be.

3 cups chopped fresh cilantro

¼ white onion, roughly chopped

4 garlic cloves

¼ cup fresh lime juice (2 or 3 limes)

3 tablespoons red wine vinegar

½ teaspoon salt

½ cup olive oil

1 In your food processor, throw together the cilantro, white onion, garlic, lime juice, red wine vinegar, and salt and pulse it until everything looks nice and mixed up. Pour in the oil and let that shit run until it looks sorta smooth. No food processor? Just mince everything into tiny pieces, mix in the vinegars and salt, then slowly stir in the oil. Easy.

2 However you made it, pour the sauce into a jar with a tight-fitting lid and let it sit for 30 minutes in the fridge or on the countertop to really develop its flavor. This will keep in the fridge for about 3 days before it loses all its brightness and isn't worth your time.

CHEAT SHEET:

We love this chimichurri with our Grilled Plantains (page 99), Summer Squash-Stuffed Flatbread (page 147), or with any of our fritters (pages 142–44).

Broiled Miso Eggplant

It's a scorching summer day in the Rio Grande Valley. A twelve-year-old boy is riding his bike back from the local farmers' market with a bag hanging from the handlebars. When he gets home, he empties the bag on the kitchen table, revealing an eggplant the size of the boy's head. As a kid, Matt's father, Byron, fucking LOVED eggplant so much, he'd use the money he earned from chores to bring home eggplant as a treat. Not ice cream, not candy. Motherfucking EGGPLANT. No wonder Matt became a vegan. Byron, this one's for you.

2 smallish eggplants, about the length of a hand

2 tablespoons grapeseed or other high-heat oil

Miso Glaze

¼ cup rice vinegar

3 tablespoons red miso

1 tablespoon Sriracha-style hot sauce

2 teaspoons toasted sesame oil

2 teaspoons maple syrup

1 Halve the eggplants lengthwise and using a knife, score a grid of small squares on the inside. Think tic-tac-toe, but you know, on an eggplant.

2 Warm a large skillet with a lid over high heat and add the grapeseed oil. If you've got one skillet large enough for all the eggplant, that's perfect; otherwise, just do this shit in stages. Put the eggplant cut side down on the skillet and scoot it around so that the eggplant doesn't stick to the pan. Cook until the flesh is browning in some places, 3 to 5 minutes. Turn the eggplant over and cover with a lid. Let this heat up until the eggplant is cooked through, another 4 to 6 minutes. If the pan starts looking a little dry, add 2 tablespoons water and cover again.

3 While the eggplant is cooking, make the miso glaze: In a small glass or bowl, mix the vinegar, miso, hot sauce, sesame oil, and maple syrup until everything looks smooth. That's it. Turn your broiler to high and let it warm up.

4 Place the cooked eggplant scored side up on a baking sheet and brush the miso glaze on top of the flesh of the eggplant until the entire surface is coated and the glaze starts getting into your score marks. Stick that all under the broiler until the miso glaze is bubbling, 3 to 4 minutes. Let this cool for a minute or two before serving.

Makes enough for 4 people / Cook time: 40 minutes

Sheet Pan Cauliflower with Pumpkin Seeds

The summer heat has finally broken, the leaves have turned from green to gold, and people are lining up at coffee shops for their pumpkin-spice lattes. But you know, there's a better way to celebrate the changing of the seasons and you don't need to sip on a cup of sugar. This roasty toasty side is chock-full of fall flavors, and let's be honest, you could use the fiber.

1 large head cauliflower, chopped into bite-size florets

4 tablespoons olive oil

2 teaspoons garlic granules

Salt and black pepper

2 tablespoons ume plum vinegar

½ teaspoon red pepper flakes

½ cup pumpkin or sunflower seeds, roasted

½ cup sliced green onions

½ lemon

1 Warm up your oven to 400°F.

2 In a large bowl, toss the cauliflower with 2 tablespoons of the olive oil, the garlic granules, and a pinch each of salt and pepper. Make sure all the cauliflower gets some love.

3 Spread all the florets out on a sheet pan in as close to one layer as you can manage. (Hold onto the bowl.) Put the pan in the oven and let those fuckers roast for 20 minutes.

4 In a small bowl, whisk together the remaining 2 tablespoons olive oil, the plum vinegar, and pepper flakes. Now you've got a few minutes to kill before the cauliflower is done. Go enjoy your life.

5 When the 20 minutes is up on the roasted cauliflower, run back to the kitchen, take the cauliflower out of the oven, and drizzle the plum vinegar dressing over it. Toss the cauliflower on the baking sheet to make sure all the pieces get coated, then stick that shit back into the oven until the cauliflower looks golden brown in some spots, another 10 to 15 minutes.

6 When it's all ready to go, transfer the cauliflower back to the bowl you first tossed it in, fold in the pumpkin seeds and green onions, and squeeze over the lemon juice. Taste and add more plum vinegar or whatever the fuck you think it needs. Serve warm or at room temperature.

Curried Red Lentil Soup

We fucking love lentils and are always dreaming up new ways to get them in our belly. They're good for you, good for the planet, and cheap as fuck. What's not to like? This soup is perfect for when you don't think you have enough shit in your fridge to prepare dinner. You'll be able to make this and feel like a damn superhero for pulling a meal out of thin air. We're applauding, we promise.

1 tablespoon olive or coconut oil

1 yellow onion, chopped

2 carrots, chopped

Salt and black pepper

1 tablespoon minced fresh ginger

1 jalapeño or similar pepper, seeded and minced

1 tablespoon no-salt yellow curry powder

1 teaspoon ground coriander

1 tablespoon tomato paste

2 cups red lentils, rinsed

7 cups vegetable broth

Juice from 1 lemon (about 2 tablespoons)

1 tablespoon ume plum vinegar

1 In a large soup pot with a lid, warm the oil over medium-high heat. Add the onion and carrots with a pinch of salt and sauté until the carrots softens up and the onion has some color on it, 5 to 8 minutes. Toss in the ginger, jalapeño, curry powder, and coriander and cook for a minute so that all the spices have some time to wake up from their slumber in your spice rack.

2 Once the kitchen smells amazing, add the tomato paste and red lentils and cook until the tomato paste has started to break down and coat the veggies and lentils. Add the vegetable broth and bring the pot to a simmer. Once it's simmering, stir the pot, throw on the lid, and reduce the heat a little. Let it cook like this, stirring occasionally, until the lentils are soft and are starting to dissolve into the soup, about 20 minutes.

3 Add the lemon juice, plum vinegar, and a little salt and pepper. Cook for another minute or two before tasting. Add more curry powder or whatever you think it needs. Serve right away.

CHEAT SHEET:

We love this soup as is, or with a dollop of our Garlic-Mint Yogurt (page 94), or with a side of Herbed Flatbreads (page 128), Morning Cornbread (page 28), or Cumin Rice (page 115). In other words, this shit goes with everything.

Makes enough for 6 people / Cook time: 35 minutes

Creamy Broccoli Soup with Peanuts and Ginger

When Michelle was broke as a joke, she basically ate broccoli, rice, and peanut sauce every damn day. This soup is a luxurious throwback to those simple but comforting meals. If you're skeptical of the peanut and broccoli combo, just know that you're fucking wrong and it's delicious. Wanna get extra full? Pair it with our Coconut Rice (page 112).

1 tablespoon olive or coconut oil

1 yellow onion, chopped

Salt

1 russet potato, peeled and chopped

1 tablespoon chopped fresh ginger

3 garlic cloves, chopped

½ teaspoon ground coriander

Grated zest of 1 lime

1 large head broccoli, chopped into florets (about 8 cups)

¼ teaspoon citric acid (optional)

5 cups vegetable broth

1 cup nondairy milk

2 tablespoons peanut butter, ideally one without a shit-ton of sugar

1 tablespoon ume plum vinegar

Black pepper

1 In a large soup pot, warm up the oil over medium-high heat. Add the onion with a pinch of salt and sauté until the onion starts to soften and look translucent, 3 to 5 minutes. Add the potato and sauté for another 2 minutes so that the potato gets all mixed up with the onions. Add the ginger, garlic, and coriander and sauté until the spices start warming up and smelling delicious, about 1 minute. Add the lime zest, broccoli, and citric acid (if using) and stir to integrate them into the pot. Pour in the veggie broth and milk. Let the pot come to a simmer, about 5 minutes.

2 Reduce the heat to medium and stir in the peanut butter, plum vinegar, and a little black pepper.

3 Now for the fun part: Grab your immersion blender, stick it right in the pot, and pulse it until three-quarters of the soup looks pureed. Stir and make sure you have the desired amount of chunks in the pot. Want it all pureed? That's cool with us, blend away. No immersion blender? Scoop three-quarters of the soup into your stand blender and let it run.

For Serving

Chopped peanuts

Fresh cilantro

Green onions

Fresh lime juice

4 Taste the soup and see what you think it needs. More lime zest? Garlic? Your call.

5 To serve, scoop some soup into a bowl and top with some chopped peanuts, fresh cilantro or green onions, and a squeeze of lime juice.

Chickpea and Tahini Soup with Orzo

This soup comes together fast, requires minimal chopping, but tastes like you spent all afternoon over the stove. The pasta, or rice if you want to make it gluten-free, needs to be cooked ahead of time. It's also a great place to use leftover rice from a previous meal. The tahini gives the broth a sorta smoky taste that will have everyone asking for more bowls and the recipe. Guard it with your life. They can't know how easy it was, k?

1 tablespoon olive oil

1 yellow onion, chopped

1 large zucchini, unpeeled, cut into quarter moons

4 garlic cloves, minced

1 teaspoon dried oregano

¼ teaspoon salt

¼ teaspoon black pepper, plus more for serving

1½ cups cooked chickpeas, or 1 can (15 ounces), drained and rinsed

8 cups vegetable broth

4 tablespoons fresh lemon juice (about 2 lemons)

2 tablespoons tahini

1 carrot, shredded on a box grater (about ½ cup)

¼ cup chopped fresh dill

¼ cup chopped fresh parsley

2 cups cooked orzo (or similarly small pasta) or rice

1 In a large soup pot, warm up the olive oil over medium heat. Add the onion and cook until you start to see it brown in some spots, about 8 minutes. Add the zucchini, garlic, and oregano and cook for another 2 minutes more, just until the zucchini starts to soften up. Throw in the salt, black pepper, chickpeas, and vegetable broth and scrape off any tasty bits of onion that might have stuck to the bottom of the pot. Let this come to a simmer, then reduce the heat to low.

2 In a medium glass, start mixing the lemon juice and tahini together as best you can. Slowly whisk in a couple tablespoons of the warm soup broth at a time until all the tahini has all dissolved into the liquid in the glass. If you try to cut this step, you'll end up with a clump of tahini siting at the bottom of your pot, so don't fucking rush this. Once the tahini is one with the liquid in the glass, incorporate it into the soup pot along with the shredded carrot, dill, and parsley (save some of the herbs for garnish). Now add 1½ cups of the cooked orzo to the pot and remove from the heat. Stir and taste, then add more of whatever the fuck you think it needs.

3 Serve warm with a little of the remaining orzo on top of each bowl with some of the reserved chopped herbs and a crack of some fresh pepper.

CHEAT SHEET:

Want to make this soup a one-pot wonder? Add 1 cup dried orzo at the same time as the chickpeas and cook until the pasta is tender. This results in a thicker soup, but it does save on dishes and time. Your call. The leftovers are delicious but super thick since the pasta will absorb a lot of the broth. Just add a little water or broth to thin it out as you reheat it.

Makes about 2 cups / Cook time: 25 minutes

Grilled Tomatillo and Avocado Salsa

You might walk by the tomatillo display every summer at your market, but you dunno what the fuck to do with them. They look like little green tomatoes with paper skin, but they're so much more. When you put them in any dish, especially salsa, they provide a certain tanginess you just can't fucking get anywhere else. This recipe is for the beginners who wanna look like pros. If you can make a smoothie, you can make salsa.

6 tomatillos, papery skins removed

1 or 2 jalapeños, depending on your love of heat

½ white onion

1 tablespoon avocado or similar neutral-tasting oil

2 garlic cloves

1 avocado, halved and pitted

1 cup vegetable broth or water

¼ cup chopped fresh cilantro

1 green onion, chopped

2 tablespoons orange juice

Juice of 2 limes (about 2 tablespoons)

Pinch of salt

1 Heat your grill up to medium-high heat.

2 In a medium bowl, toss the tomatillos, jalapeño, and white onion with the oil until they all have a lil' bit on them. Place the tomatillos, jalapeños, and onion (cut side down) on the grill, however they will stay. Cook the tomatillos until they get some grill marks on them, turning onto each side until they soften up, about 8 minutes total. Do the same with the onion and jalapeños until they are covered in grill marks and the peppers' skins are blistered in some spots.

3 Let the grilled items cool for a few minutes. Scoop the avocado into a blender or food processor. Add the grilled vegetables, vegetable broth, cilantro, green onion, orange juice, lime juice, and salt. Run until you get your desired salsa consistency. You know what you like. Taste and add more of whatever the fuck you think it needs.

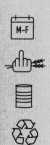

Red Pepper Rice

Ya know how most people eat the same four fucking things over and over again? This just became your fifth. This is a catch-all side that goes great with just about anything. For a dish that doesn't have any cream, this shit is impossibly velvety. We love it as part of a brunch spread with our Poblano Home Fries (page 38) and Everyday Tofu Scramble (page 20) or as part of dinner alongside our Sunday Beans (page 155) and Everyday Cabbage Slaw (page 67).

2 roasted red bell peppers,* or 1 jar (10 ounces), drained

2 tablespoons tomato paste

½ white onion, chopped

4 garlic cloves, chopped

Juice of 1 lemon (about 2 tablespoons)

½ teaspoon salt

¼ cup olive oil

2 cups basmati or other long-grain rice, rinsed

1¾ cups vegetable broth

1 tablespoon nutritional yeast (nooch) or more to taste

¼ cup minced fresh chives (optional)

*See the Field Guide, opposite.

1 Throw the roasted red peppers, tomato paste, onion, garlic, lemon juice, and salt in a food processor or blender and run that shit until it's looking smooth-ish. You want to have around 1½ cups of bell pepper mixture. This can be done ahead of time if you want to have it waiting in the fridge come dinnertime.

2 When you are ready for some rice, heat up a large pot with a lid over medium-high heat and add the oil. Add the rice and sauté until all the grains are coated and it starts to smell a little toasty, about 5 minutes. This is a crucial step, so don't half-ass it. Just wait the 5 minutes, k?

3 Pour in the blended bell pepper mix and veggie broth, stir, and bring the pot to a simmer. Once it's bubbling, reduce the heat to low, stir, and throw on the lid. Let this cook until the rice is tender and the liquid is all absorbed, about 20 minutes. Set a timer so you don't forget that shit.

4 Once the rice is cooked, pull off the lid, sprinkle with the nutritional yeast, and fluff the top of the rice with a fork. Put a clean kitchen towel between the pot and the lid and let the rice steam for another 10 minutes. This helps the rice be extra fluffy and delicious, but if you are in a hurry, you can definitely skip this.

5 When you are ready to serve, fold in the chives if you want. Taste and add more lemon juice or whatever it needs.

FIELD GUIDE:
ROASTING PEPPERS

You don't need to spend $10 on some jarred roasted peppers when you can absolutely do this yourself. It's easy. Grab some foil and peppers and get your ass to the stove. These cooking methods are perfect for big, sweeter peppers like bell peppers, poblanos, and large banana peppers.

GAS STOVE

PLACE A PEPPER ON THE BURNER OF A GAS STOVE AND TURN THE HEAT TO HIGH. BURN THE SHIT OUT OF THE SKIN OF THE PEPPER, ROTATING IT UNTIL EVERY SIDE IS BLACKENED. THIS WHOLE PROCESS WILL TAKE ABOUT 8 MINUTES.

ELECTRIC STOVE

TURN YOUR BROILER TO HIGH AND PLACE THE PEPPERS ON THE RACK CLOSEST TO THE HEAT SOURCE. TURN THEM EVERY COUPLE MINUTES UNTIL EVERY SIDE IS BLACKENED, ABOUT 10 MINUTES.

When the peppers are blackened all over, place each one in a piece of foil and wrap it up tight so that no steam can escape. Let them sit and cool for 15 minutes. When the peppers have cooled, the burnt skin will have separated from the flesh of the pepper. You should be able to peel that shit off no problem. Don't run the pepper under the tap thinking you are saving time. You will lose some of the awesome roasted flavor, so don't fuck things up now. Once the peppers are cleaned, go make something badass. You can do this shit a day or two in advance. Just keep them in the fridge.

Coconut Rice

Coconut and rice deserve the same respect other classic culinary pairings get. Red sauce and pasta, peanut butter and jelly, potatoes and ketchup. The coconut milk brings a buttery richness to the fluffy carb-liciousness of rice. Together, they equal something greater than the sum of their parts.

2 tablespoons coconut or olive oil

1 shallot, minced, or ¼ cup minced white onion

Salt

2 cups jasmine rice, rinsed

1½ cups full-fat coconut milk or one can (15 ounces)

2¼ cups vegetable broth

Grated zest and juice of 1 lime (about 1 tablespoon juice)

¼ cup minced green onions or chives (optional)

1 Warm up the oil in a large pot with a lid over medium-high heat. Add the shallot and sauté that shit with a pinch of salt until it starts to look translucent, about 3 minutes. Add the rice and continue sautéing until the rice gets a little golden and starts smelling kinda nutty, about 5 more minutes. Add the coconut milk, vegetable broth, and lime zest, and bring the pot to a gentle boil.

2 Once the pot is boiling, stir, then reduce the heat to low and slap on that lid. Let this cook for 20 minutes and try to leave that shit alone. Once the 20 minutes are up, check to make sure that the rice is tender and all the liquid has been absorbed.

3 Drizzle with the lime juice and sprinkle on ½ teaspoon salt, then fluff the rice with a fork to work the salt and lime juice in. Put a clean kitchen towel between the pot and the lid and let the rice steam for another 10 minutes. This helps the rice be extra fluffy and delicious, but if you are in a hurry, you can definitely skip this. Fold in the green onions if you want. Serve warm or at room temperature.

FIELD GUIDE:
WASHING RICE

If you're a lifelong rice lover, then this is old news, but if you're new to the rice game, listen up: YOU SHOULD ALWAYS WASH YOUR RICE. We don't care if the recipes don't tell you to. WASH YOUR RICE. White rice is just brown rice with its outer layer polished off. This process creates a lot of extra-starchy powder that clings to the kernels. When you wash the rice, that surface starch rinses away with the water, making the resulting pot of rice fluffier and less likely to clump together. Brown rice may not have this extra starch lying around it, but it can still benefit from a wash because grit and who knows what else can be mixed in there.

To wash your rice, pour your measured amount into a fine-mesh sieve and run it under the sink as you swirl the rice around with your hands until the water running out looks relatively clear. You can also pour your measured rice into a large bowl, cover it with water, and swish it around with your fingers to help dislodge that starch. Pour it through a mesh sieve to drain and rinse it again under the sink to rinse off any remaining starch. Either way you do it, the result is a better pot of rice for less than 2 minutes of extra work.

eat the rich
with ♥ AND
TAJIN LIMON

Cumin Rice

This is barely a recipe, but knowing lots of different ways to cook rice is handy as hell when you're throwing together a meal. Plus, it's a cost-effective way to stretch your food budget even further with stuff you probably already have on hand. Trust us, we're probably eating rice right now.

1 tablespoon olive or coconut oil

2 teaspoons cumin seeds

2 bay leaves

2 cups basmati rice, rinsed

Salt

3¾ cups water

Chopped cilantro or green onions, for garnish

1 In a large pot with a lid, warm up the oil over medium heat. Add the cumin seeds and sauté them around until they start making little sputtering or popping noises, no longer than a minute. Add the bay leaves and rice and cook together for a minute or so, just to get everything mixed together. Add a pinch of salt and the water and let it come to a simmer.

2 Once the pot is simmering, stir, reduce the heat to low, and cover. Let this cook for 15 minutes with the lid on. Once the 15 minutes is up, take off the lid and fluff the rice with a fork. Sprinkle on a little more salt and then put a clean kitchen towel between the pot and the lid and let the rice steam for another 10 minutes, covered. This helps the rice get nice and fluffy, but if you're in a rush, it's okay to skip this step. Uncover, fold in any chopped herbs you're using, such as cilantro and green onions, and serve right away.

Makes about 4 cups / Cook time: 45 minutes

Cilantro Rice

Stop giving that assembly-line, mediocre burrito spot your money for a bowl you can make yourself. Throw together this rice at home and add some veggies and protein like our Sunday Beans (page 155). Charge yourself extra for guac if you want the full experience.

1½ cups chopped fresh cilantro

¼ cup chopped green onion

1 jalapeño, chopped

4 garlic cloves, chopped

½ cup fresh lime juice (about 6 to 8 limes)

½ teaspoon salt

¼ cup olive oil

½ white onion, diced

2 cups long-grain white rice

1½ cups vegetable broth or water

1 Throw the cilantro, green onion, jalapeño, garlic, lime juice, and salt in a food processor or blender. Run that shit until you've got a green sauce thing going. Set it aside.

2 In a large pot with a lid, heat up the olive oil over medium-high heat. Add the onion and sauté until it starts to look translucent, 3 to 5 minutes, then throw in the rice. Sauté all that around until the onion and rice start to look a little golden brown, about 5 minutes. Yeah, it's an extra step, but it makes the rice come out so fucking good that you'll never, ever regret it.

3 Add the veggie broth and green sauce and stir. Let this come to a simmer, then reduce the heat to low and throw on the lid. Let this the fuck alone until the rice is tender and the liquid is all absorbed, about 20 minutes. Set a timer so you don't forget that shit.

4 When your rice is cooked, remove from the heat and taste. Add whatever the fuck you think it needs, then put a clean kitchen towel between the pot and the lid and let the rice steam for another 10 minutes. This helps the rice be extra fluffy and delicious, but if you are in a hurry, you can definitely skip this. Serve warm or at room temperature.

CHEAT SHEET:

Cilantro is one of the few herbs where the stems have the same taste as the leaves. So, if you don't mind a little extra crunch, just chop up the whole bunch without trying to pick out only the leaves. Not only does this make prep way faster, you also get like double your money's worth. More money and more time? You're fucking welcome.

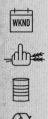

Makes about 2 cups, enough for 4 to 6 people / Cook time: 1½ hours, mostly inactive

Yellow Split Pea Dip

If you've mastered our 5-Minute Hummus (page 92), consider this your next assignment. This Santorini staple is a helluva lot more accessible than the island and cheaper. Plus, it's not a crowded wasteland of influencers trying to get that iconic Greece vacation photo. Save the trip, make the dip. It's great with our Herbed Flatbreads (page 128) or any of our fritters (see pages 142–44).

3 tablespoons olive oil, divided

½ red onion, diced

2 garlic cloves, minced

¼ teaspoon dried oregano

2¼ cups vegetable broth or water

1 cup yellow split peas, rinsed

1 bay leaf

½ teaspoon salt

¼ teaspoon paprika

2 tablespoons fresh lemon juice (about 1 lemon)

For Topping

Paprika

Minced red onion

Roughly chopped capers

Olive oil

1 Warm up 1 tablespoon of the olive oil in a large saucepan over medium-high heat. Add the onion and sauté that around until it starts to look a little golden in some spots, 5 to 7 minutes. Add the garlic and oregano and sauté for another minute until the garlic starts smelling good. Add the veggie broth, split peas, and bay leaf and let that pot come to a rolling boil. Reduce the heat to medium-low and let the pot simmer until the peas are soft, another 20 to 25 minutes. We're gonna blend this up, so if you're not sure if they're ready, just keep cooking them until they're mushy. You're not gonna fuck this up.

2 When the peas are soft, remove from the heat and pull out the bay leaf. Sprinkle in the salt, paprika, and lemon juice, and add the remaining 2 tablespoons olive oil to the pot. Then, using an immersion blender, puree the mixture right in the pot until smooth. No immersion blender? Throw it right into your blender or food processor and run it until it's smooth. If it looks a little thick or you're having trouble blending it, add some more veggie broth to get things going, a couple tablespoons at a time. This is gonna thicken up in the fridge a lot, so if it's looking too thin, don't stress. Stick this pot in the fridge to cool completely.

3 To serve, scoop out some of the split pea dip and top with paprika, some minced red onion, and chopped capers. Drizzle with a little olive oil and watch the compliments roll in.

CHEAT SHEET:

Want to make this dip into a simple Santorini
Split Pea Soup? After you puree it in the pot, add
another 1½ cups veggie broth or so until you get
the desired consistency. Serve warm topped with
caramelized onions and a little paprika. You can
use this same method to finish up any leftover dip
you have. It's fucking easy and so, so good.

Makes enough for 6 people / Cook time: 1 hour, mostly inactive

Farro and Red Bean Soup

This soup is so comforting and filling that you will find yourself making it as soon as the temperature drops below 50°F. Farro is a kind of old-timey variety of wheat that is similar in texture to barley. It's chewy, delicious, and adds an extra silkiness to the soup while it's cooking. It can be hard to find non-pearled farro (meaning whole grain, with its bran layer intact) in North America, but if you do, just increase the simmer time by another 15 minutes and you'll be good to go. Can't find farro? Sub in barley and let soup season begin.

2 tablespoons olive oil

1 yellow onion, chopped

Salt

2 celery ribs, chopped

1 carrot, chopped

5 cremini mushrooms, cut into bite-size pieces

2 tablespoons chopped fresh rosemary

1 tablespoon tomato paste

4 garlic gloves, minced

2 tablespoons nutritional yeast (nooch)

1 teaspoon dried thyme

½ teaspoon red pepper flakes

1 cup farro, rinsed

1 can (15 ounces) crushed tomatoes, preferably fire-roasted

1 In a large stockpot or soup pot, warm up the olive oil over medium-high heat. Add the onion with a pinch of salt and sauté until you start to see it brown in some spots, about 8 minutes. Add the celery and carrot and cook until everything has really softened up, another 5 minutes. Toss in the mushrooms and rosemary and cook just until the mushrooms start to soften too, about 3 minutes. Look at you, building flavors. Let's keep that shit up.

2 Stir in the tomato paste, garlic, nooch, thyme, pepper flakes, and farro. Make sure that the tomato paste isn't in some giant clump and that everything looks well mixed. Add the crushed tomatoes and red beans, stir, and pour in the vegetable broth. Bring the pot to a low simmer and let it cook, stirring occasionally, until the farro is soft, about 30 minutes.

1½ cups cooked red or kidney beans, or 1 can (15 ounces), drained and rinsed

8 cups vegetable broth

1 bunch Swiss chard or kale, midribs removed and leaves cut into ribbons (about 6 cups)

1 tablespoon red wine vinegar

1 tablespoon ume plum vinegar

¼ cup chopped fresh parsley

Black pepper

Crusty bread, Morning Cornbread (page 28), or Throwback Dinner Rolls (page 133), for serving

3 Once the farro is tender, add the Swiss chard, red wine vinegar, and plum vinegar. Cook for another couple minutes, just until the greens are tender to your liking. Stir in the parsley and season with a little salt and black pepper. Taste and add more of whatever you think it might need like nooch or more salt.

4 Serve right away with some crusty bread, our cornbread, or our dinner rolls. The farro will absorb some of the broth as the leftovers sit so just add a little extra broth or water when you reheat it. This will keep beautifully for up to 3 days in the fridge before the chard starts looking a little worn out.

HERBED
FLATBREADS
(PAGE 128)

CALIFORNIA
GARDEN
DRESSING AND
SIDE SALAD
(PAGE 56)

CHICKEN FINGER
SHROOMS (OPPOSITE)

5-MINUTE HUMMUS
(PAGE 92)

Chicken Finger Shrooms

Look, we know you saw "shrooms" and almost flipped the page. Neither one of us particularly likes mushrooms, but these crispy morsels stand in a category all their own. They are solid enough to be an appetizer, and you can add them to a salad or sandwich them into flatbread with some hummus. Just trust us and we'll make a believer out of you, too.

2 clusters oyster or hen of the woods (maitake) mushrooms

1 tablespoon safflower oil or other high-heat oil

Salt and black pepper

Seasoned Flour

1 cup all-purpose flour

1 cup cornmeal

1 teaspoon dried oregano

1 tablespoon garlic powder

1 tablespoon onion powder

1 tablespoon paprika

1 teaspoon ground ginger

1 teaspoon salt

2 teaspoons black pepper

2 cups beer, whatever kind you drink, or club soda

Safflower oil or other high-heat oil, for frying

For Serving

Ketchup, BBQ sauce, or Cashew Buttermilk Dressing (page 88)

1 Rinse the mushrooms and cut the clusters in quarters so you have at least 8 tight clusters in total. Random pieces might fall off, and that's cool. Cook those lil' fuckers, too.

2 Heat up a large skillet over medium-high heat and pour in the 1 tablespoon oil. Throw the mushrooms in, sprinkle them with some salt and pepper, and put something heavy on top of them so they flatten while they sear. Something like a smaller pan or even a brick wrapped in foil would work. We want all that water in the mushrooms to get the fuck out so we can put some flavor in there, kinda like how we tell y'all to cook tofu. After 3 to 4 minutes, they should look seared and browned in some places and, ya know, flattened. Flip and repeat. When they're done, put the mushrooms on a plate to cool while you mix up the rest of the ingredients.

3 Make the seasoned flour: In a shallow medium bowl, mix together the flour, cornmeal, oregano, garlic powder, onion powder, paprika, ground ginger, salt, and pepper until that shit looks uniform and smells good. Set it aside.

4 When ready to fry, pour the beer into another shallow medium bowl. Dunk the cooked mushrooms in the beer and then toss them in the seasoned flour until they're all covered. Place them on a plate.

(recipe continues)

5 Line a large plate with paper towels. Heat about 1 inch of oil in that same large skillet over medium heat. Drop in a few sprinkles of flour to make sure it's hot enough. When the flour sizzles without burning the fuck up, you know it's ready. Working in batches of about 4 pieces at a time, fry the battered mushrooms until the edges start to look golden brown, 2 to 3 minutes on each side depending on how hot your pan is. Transfer them to the paper towels to drain and keep them warm by covering lightly with another plate or a sheet of foil until the all the batches are fried up.

6 Serve these guys warm or at room temperature with ketchup, BBQ sauce, or our Cashew Buttermilk Dressing (page 88).

CHEAT SHEET:

These chicken finger shrooms are also great tucked into pita or our Herbed Flatbreads (page 128) with some 5-Minute Hummus (page 92), lots of herbs and veggies, and our California Garden Dressing and Side Salad (page 56). Hell, they're even good for breakfast with some gravy and a biscuit. You can't miss.

Braised Greens

This is a great way to get your greens with minimal effort. The braising process really brings a depth of flavor that you won't get through sautéing alone. When it's too cold for a salad, we've got you covered.

2 tablespoons olive or coconut oil

½ yellow onion, chopped

2 large bunches of kale and/or collard greens, tough midribs removed, leaves chopped (about 8 cups)

6 garlic cloves, minced

1 tablespoon Bragg Liquid Aminos or soy sauce

1 teaspoon ume plum vinegar

2 cups vegetable broth

1 tablespoon fresh lemon juice

Salt and black pepper

1 Add the olive oil to a large soup pot with a lid over medium-high heat. Once hot, add the onion and sauté until softened and lightly browned, 5 to 8 minutes. Add the greens a couple handfuls at a time, tossing them with the onions and oil as you go. Once you've got all the greens in the pot, add the garlic, liquid aminos, and plum vinegar and stir to make sure everything looks mixed up.

2 Add the vegetable broth, stir again, cover the pot, and reduce the heat to medium-low. Cook, stirring every now and then, until the greens are tender, 25 to 30 minutes. A gentle simmer is fine, but anything more will overcook your greens, so keep that heat on the lower side, k?

3 Once they're almost how you like them, uncover, increase the heat to medium-high, and cook, stirring often, until some more of the liquid from the pot has evaporated, no longer than 5 minutes. Remove from the heat, add the lemon juice and a little salt and pepper. Taste and add more of whatever you think it needs. Serve warm.

CHEAT SHEET:

Serve the greens as is or topped with our Onion Croutons (page 58). We love these alongside our Morning Cornbread, with our Dirty Rice with Lentils (page 162), or as a side to our Pepper Cheese Hoagies (page 80) or White Mac and Cheese (page 177). Hell, we've even tossed them with plain pasta, covered the whole thing in nutritional yeast, and eaten it for dinner. They're that good.

Makes enough for 4 to 6 people / Cook time: 35 minutes

Sunshine Pasta Salad

Remember the first time you had pasta salad that was so good your pupils dilated? Welcome back.

1 pound pasta, such as macaroni or shells

Dressing

12 ounces soft silken tofu*

½ cup nondairy milk

½ cup nondairy sour cream

3 tablespoons olive oil

2 tablespoons brown sugar

2 tablespoons apple cider vinegar

½ teaspoon salt

½ teaspoon paprika

½ teaspoon ground turmeric

½ teaspoon garlic granules

½ teaspoon onion powder

Black pepper

Salad

1 tablespoon apple cider vinegar

1 cup shredded carrots

½ cup chopped red onion

½ cup chopped green onion

*You want the kind of silken tofu that's shelf-stable, not the stuff packed in water in the cold case. You'll find it near the soy sauce at most grocery stores.

1 Cook the pasta according to the package directions.

2 While those fuckers are cooking, make the dressing: Throw the tofu, milk, sour cream, olive oil, brown sugar, apple cider vinegar, salt, paprika, turmeric, garlic granules, onion powder, and pepper to taste in a blender or food processor and run that shit until it looks smooth and all the spices are mixed in.

3 When the pasta is done, drain it and run it under cool water to stop the cooking. Pour the cooled pasta into a large bowl and toss it with the 2 tablespoons of apple cider vinegar.

4 Assemble the salad: Add half the dressing to the pasta and toss until it's all coated. Add the carrots, red onion, green onion, and a little more dressing and toss again. Taste and add more dressing to get it how you like it. Serve right away.

CHEAT SHEET:

This salad is best when it's tossed together before it's served. Making it for a party? Prepare the dressing ahead of time, let it chill in the fridge, and add it to the pasta and veggies right before you throw it on that picnic table and never look back.

Makes about 8 flatbreads, enough for 4 people / Cook time: 1½ hours, mostly inactive

Herbed Flatbreads

Felt left out when everyone started making sourdough loaves because you don't how to make bread? Well, this is just the recipe your yeast-phobic ass has been waiting for. You will not mess this up, and everyone will be shocked by how good these flatbreads are. Don't tell them your secrets. Let the curiosity kill them.

¾ cup warm water

½ cup nondairy yogurt

1 envelope (2¼ teaspoons) active dry yeast

2½ cups all-purpose or whole wheat pastry flour, plus more for rolling

1 teaspoon garlic powder (optional if you're a hater)

½ teaspoon salt

Spray oil

2 to 3 tablespoons minced fresh herbs, such as dill, basil, rosemary, chives, and parsley

1 In a small bowl, whisk together the warm water, yogurt, and yeast. If it starts looking foamy in a minute or two, then your yeast is alive and you can proceed. If not, your water wasn't warm. It was fucking hot and you committed yeast murder. Start again until you get it right.

2 In a large bowl, stir together the flour, garlic powder (if using), and salt. Pour that warm, watery yogurt mixture into the flour and stir until a shaggy pile of dough comes together. If that shit still looks super dry, add more water a tablespoon at a time until it holds together better.

3 Knead the dough in the bowl until it comes together into a ball without a bunch of dry spots, less than 5 minutes. Spray it with a little oil, then cover it and let it rise in a warm spot until it almost doubles in size, about 1 hour.

4 Once the dough has risen, punch that motherfucker down to deflate it, then turn the dough out onto a floured surface. Sprinkle the dough with the herbs and knead them into the dough until you feel like they're mixed up evenly. You don't want all that flavor bunched together in one spot. Next, flatten the dough out a little, then cut it into 8 equal-ish pieces. You can fire this shit up now or stick these in the fridge, tightly covered, for up to 24 hours, before cooking them. Just give them 10 minutes to warm up on the counter before moving on to the next step.

5 To cook the flatbreads, roll out each piece on a well-floured surface so it doesn't stick. Warm up a large sauté pan over medium-high heat and make sure it's nice and hot before you flop the dough in there. Once it's hot, spray the pan lightly with oil, then place the rolled-out dough right in. Cook for 1 to 2 minutes. Bubbles will start appearing in the dough and that's perfect. Once the bottom looks golden brown, flip that shit, and continue cooking until the dough looks cooked through, golden brown in some spots, and fucking delicious. Keep going until you run out of dough. Serve warm or at room temperature. These keep well in a sealed bag for up to 3 days for maximum deliciousness.

CHEAT SHEET:

We love this as a base for our Hippie Hummus Wraps (page 59) and as the base for the fancy version of our Summer Squash-Stuffed Flatbread (page 147). It's great alongside any big salad or as a flatbread on a mezze board with our 5-Minute Hummus (page 92), some fresh veggies, and some olives.

White Bean Soup with Rolled Herb Dumplings

This is an updated, streamlined take on our viral Chickpea and Dumplings recipe from our first book. We've changed the veggies and herbs, subbed in some new beans, and made the whole cooking process way fucking easier. But the taste? Hot damn. This is one of our favorite soups in this book. These dumplings would make even Michelle's nana proud, and she was one tough customer.

Herb Dumplings

1½ cups all-purpose flour

1 tablespoon nutritional yeast (nooch)

1½ teaspoons garlic powder

¼ teaspoon salt

1 tablespoon olive oil

¼ cup minced fresh chives

¼ cup minced fresh dill and/ or parsley

½ cup nondairy milk

Bean Soup

¼ cup olive oil

1 yellow onion, chopped

3 celery ribs, chopped

2 parsnips, chopped

1 carrot, chopped

Pinch of salt

1 teaspoon garlic powder

½ teaspoon dried oregano

½ cup dry white wine or vegetable broth

1 First, make the dumplings: Add the flour to a medium bowl and whisk in the nooch, garlic powder, and salt. Make a well in the center of the flour and dump in the oil, minced herbs, and milk. Slowly stir everything together until you get a shaggy ball of dough, then knead it a few times in the bowl until you get together a dough without huge dry spots. If the dough feels a little too dry, knead in more milk, a tablespoon at a time, until you get the right consistency.

2 On a well-floured surface, roll out the dough about ⅛ inch thick. Think super-thin-crust pizza. Cut the dumplings into pieces about 1 inch wide and no longer than 1½ inches long. You want them to be able to fit in a spoon. Stack them up on a floured plate and stick them in the fridge, uncovered, while you make the rest of the soup.

3 Now it's time for the bean soup: In a large soup pot, heat the olive oil over medium heat. Add the onion and sauté until it starts to brown in some places, 5 to 7 minutes. Add the celery, parsnips, carrot, and salt and cook until the veggies start to soften, another 3 to 4 minutes. Add the garlic powder and oregano and cook for another minute.

(recipe and ingredients continue)

¼ cup all-purpose flour

8 cups vegetable broth

3 garlic cloves, minced

1½ cups cooked small white beans, or 1 can (15 ounces), drained and rinsed

8 kale leaves, midribs removed, leaves roughly chopped

¼ cup minced fresh chives

¼ cup minced fresh dill and/or parsley

Juice of ½ lemon

Black pepper

4 Splash in the wine and use it to scrape off whatever onions or seasonings have stuck to the bottom of the pot. Sprinkle with the flour, then start whisking it in with the veggies and oil still in the pot. It should look a little like clumps of paste forming in the pan. You're not fucking up. Keep whisking that shit around until it smells kinda nutty and looks a little toasted, about 1 minute. Slowly whisk in the veggie broth, 2 cups at a time, making sure everything is well incorporated and smooth before pouring in more. Basically, don't allow any dough clumps to form from this point on and you'll be good. Once all the broth is in the pot, add the garlic and let the soup come to a simmer, stirring occasionally, and scraping the bottom to make sure nothing is stuck. You'll feel the broth sort of thicken up as it comes to a simmer.

5 Once the pot is at a simmer, add the dumplings. Add a couple at time so they don't get all stuck together in a giant glob of dough and ruin your whole night. Just take it slow—you're almost fucking done. Once the dumplings are all in, gently stir them around once so that the broth covers everybody. Let them simmer together for 3 minutes to give the pot a chance to warm back up. Add the white beans and kale and let that all simmer together for 8 to 10 minutes so that all the dumplings have time to cook through.

6 Remove from the heat and throw in the fresh herbs, lemon juice, and some salt and pepper. Taste that shit and see if you want more herbs, spices, or salt. Serve immediately. The dumplings will absorb a lot of the broth if you have leftovers, so just add a little water or extra broth as you reheat it. The taste remains perfection though.

Throwback Dinner Rolls

Michelle grew up eating rolls like this every Thanksgiving at her Aunt Lynda's. She'd post out by the oven and get first dibs on the seemingly endless amount of pillowy goodness leaving the oven. While she can't put away tray after tray like she used to, these are the only rolls that will do when the craving hits. We love these with soup like our Farro and Red Bean Soup (page 120), as a side along with our 30-Minute Marinara (page 139), or just by themselves.

1 envelope (2¼ teaspoons) active dry yeast

1¼ cups nondairy milk, warmed but not hot

¾ teaspoon salt

3½ cups all-purpose flour, plus more for dusting

¼ cup maple syrup

2 tablespoons olive oil

1 teaspoon apple cider vinegar

Nondairy butter and flour, for the pans

Nondairy butter, melted

1 In a small glass, mix together the yeast and the warm milk. Remember, if that shit is too hot, you'll kill the yeast, so aim for something that feels like lukewarm bath water. Set that aside.

2 In a medium bowl, whisk together the salt and flour. In a large bowl (or in the bowl of your stand mixer), whisk together the maple syrup, olive oil, and apple cider vinegar. Add the milk and yeast mixture and whisk until everything looks all mixed up.

3 With a wooden spoon (or with the stand mixer on low), stir the flour mixture into the yeast mixture until a shaggy dough forms. Knead this dough on a well-floured surface (or in the mixer with the dough hook) for 5 minutes until the dough starts to look like a smooth ball. If you're kneading by hand this might take closer to 10 minutes, but you'll be getting strong as fuck. Place the dough in a greased bowl and cover it with a clean kitchen towel. Let it rise in a warm place until it's doubled in size, about 1 hour.

(recipe continues)

4 Once the dough is looking good, grab a standard round 9-inch cake or springform pan and grease and flour it. Set the pan aside for a sec. Punch down the risen dough and turn it onto a floured surface. Cut up the dough into about 7 to 8 equal pieces pieces, depending on how large you like your rolls, and attempt to keep the pieces relatively the same size. Form each piece into a ball by pulling and tucking the edges of the dough underneath itself as though you're twisting the end of a bag of bread closed. This will help you create surface tension, so you get a better rise and texture for your rolls. Gently roll the piece of dough, seam side down, on a well- floured surface to create a smooth ball. You basically make a little cage with your hand over the ball of dough and gently roll it around with as little

pressure as you can manage. The motion is very similar to using a mouse on an old computer (*stares in elder millennial*). Try it. You'll get the hang of it, we swear. Place the rolls seam side down into the prepared pan. Cover them again and let them rise until they look puffy and gorgeous, another 25 to 30 minutes.

5 Warm your oven up to 375°F.

6 Brush the risen rolls with some melted nondairy butter and toss them in the oven. Immediately bring the temperature in the oven down to 350°F and bake the rolls until the tops are golden brown, 15 to 20 minutes.

7 Brush the warm rolls with some of the leftover butter and let them cool for a few minutes before diving in.

CHEAT SHEET:

Transform these rolls to match your meal by adding aromatics like rosemary or minced garlic to the melted butter that you brush on them or folding the aromatics into the rolls as you shape them after the first rise. The possibilities are fucking endless.

Dig

Main Dishes and Entrées Worth Sharing

Cheater Beans

When you don't have time to cook beans from scratch and just need a creamy protein to round out your plate, these beans have your back. They taste like you spent all day cooking, but you can throw these together in no time. They are wonderful inside of our Green Enchiladas (page 171), alongside our Red Chilaquiles (page 40), inside our Savory Breakfast Hand Pies (page 30), or smeared onto a tortilla with a little salsa. If you have beans, you'll always have something for dinner.

1 tablespoon olive oil

1 shallot or ¼ onion, minced

Pinch of salt

2 cans (15 ounces each) beans, such as black beans, drained and rinsed

½ teaspoon ground cumin

½ teaspoon garlic powder

¼ teaspoon paprika

1 can (5 ounces) green chiles

Juice of 1 lime

1 In a medium saucepan, warm up the oil over medium-high heat. Add the shallot and salt and sauté until the shallot starts to soften, about 5 minutes. Add the beans, cumin, garlic powder, paprika, chiles, and lime juice. Stir for 2 minutes so that all the flavors get a chance to meet.

2 Grab your immersion blender and pulse that shit right in the pot until most of the beans are nice and creamy, or throw them in your blender or food processor for the same effect. Taste and add more of whatever the fuck you think it needs. Serve warm.

30-Minute Marinara

You gotta have a solid, from-scratch marinara in your repertoire. This one is as delicious as it is easy. Stop searching, you found it. Now commit this shit to memory.

3 tablespoons olive oil

½ sweet onion, finely chopped

Salt

Pinch of red pepper flakes (optional)

1 teaspoon dried oregano

1 can (28 ounces) crushed tomatoes

1 jar (24 ounces) tomato passata*

3 garlic cloves

2 tablespoons nutritional yeast (nooch)

¼ cup red wine (optional), whatever you'd pair with the sauce is fine

Salt

*Tomato passata is a tomato puree that has been strained of seeds and skins. This shit is probably hiding right by the rest of the tomato products at the grocery store. You just haven't noticed. We like it here because most of the time, the tomatoes have not been cooked, which gives the resulting sauce a brighter, sweeter taste. Can't find it? Just sub in tomato sauce and stop stressing.

1 In a large pot, warm up the oil over medium-high heat. Add the onion and a pinch of salt and cook until they start to look golden in some spots, 8 to 10 minutes.

2 Sprinkle in the pepper flakes (if using) and oregano and cook for another minute more. Stir in the crushed tomatoes and passata and reduce the heat to medium. Grab a Microplane or the smallest side of your box grater and grate the garlic cloves right into the pot as it starts to simmer. Stir in the nooch and wine (if using) and let this simmer for 5 minutes so that the flavors can really get acquainted. Now taste and add salt or whatever you think it needs. You can let this stay warm on the stove for a while, but this is all done.

CHEAT SHEET:

We serve this sauce with whatever kind of pasta we have lying around tossed with a bunch of fresh basil, but it's equally delicious spread on a pizza. Or, if you wanna really live large over a weekend, serve this alongside our Eggplant Polpetti (page 178), or with some bread, or tossed over some bucatini. You can't see it because this is a book, but we're doing a chef's kiss with the pinched hand thing.

Makes enough for 4 people / Cook time: 30 minutes

Falafel Waffle

Waffles have been stuck in sweet mode for too long. If you go through all the trouble of buying a waffle iron, you should be using that shit as often as possible. Here's an entrée that lets you get all the deliciousness of falafel flavors without having to deep fry a damn thing. Waffles are the answer.

3 cups cooked chickpeas or 2 cans (15 ounces each), drained and rinsed

½ red onion, chopped

Grated zest of 1 lemon

¼ cup fresh lemon juice (about 2 lemons)

2 tablespoons olive oil

2 teaspoons ground cumin

2 teaspoons smoked paprika

1 teaspoon ground cardamom or more cumin

1 teaspoon garlic powder

½ teaspoon salt

½ teaspoon black pepper

½ cup chopped fresh parsley

½ cup chopped fresh cilantro

2 teaspoons baking powder

2 tablespoons ground flaxseeds

¼ cup cornstarch

For Serving

Tahini Cucumber Sauce (page 93) or 5-Minute Hummus (page 92)

Tomatoes, cut up

Chopped herbs

Red onion, chopped

1 First, make sure you have a waffle maker and didn't let someone borrow it and forget to get it back. Mine has gone somewhere at the moment, so I know what the fuck I'm talking about.

2 Next, grab your food processor and throw in the chickpeas, red onion, lemon zest, lemon juice, olive oil, spices, garlic powder, salt, and pepper. Run that shit until a sorta chunky batter comes together. Add the parsley and cilantro and pulse it just long enough to work the herbs through the batter without pureeing them. Dump the blended chickpea batter into a medium bowl and sprinkle on the baking powder, flaxseeds, and cornstarch. Stir until everything is all mixed up and there aren't any big dry spots.

3 Now you've got to follow the directions for your waffle iron to cook this shit. The batter is thick, so you'll have to spread it a little with a spoon before closing the iron. Cook until all the sides are crispy, about 8 minutes depending on the machine. You can keep the cooked waffles warm in an oven set at 200°F while you cook the rest.

4 Serve them warm with some tahini sauce or hummus, cut-up tomatoes, herbs, red onion, or whatever sounds good to you.

Makes 18 to 20 small fritters, depending on the size /
Cook time: 25 minutes on the stovetop, or 30 minutes in the oven

Quinoa Zucchini Fritters

Fritters are a great way to make a lot of something quickly. Kids love them because they can dip these in their favorite sauce. You'll love them because you're sneaking veggies onto the plate of otherwise picky eaters. We've given you the option to pan-fry them on the stovetop or bake them in the oven, so do whatever feels right to you. They're delicious either way.

1½ cups cooked quinoa*

1 cup shredded zucchini or similar squash

½ cup minced white onion

¼ cup chopped fresh basil, dill, or parsley

¼ cup minced Kalamata olives or ½ teaspoon salt

3 tablespoons ground flaxseeds

2 tablespoons nutritional yeast (nooch)

1 teaspoon garlic powder

Juice of 1 lemon (about 2 tablespoons)

2 tablespoons olive oil

Neutral oil, such as avocado, or olive oil spray

*Don't know shit about quinoa or how to cook it? Check out page 220.

1 Grab a large bowl and combine the quinoa, zucchini, onion, basil, and olives until everything is nice and mixed up. Sprinkle in the ground flaxseeds, nooch, and garlic powder and then drizzle in the lemon juice and olive oil. Mix that shit up until everything kinda starts sticking together and there are no dry spots.

2 To pan-fry: Warm up a griddle or skillet over medium-high heat and add a few teaspoons of oil to prevent sticking. Scoop up about 2 tablespoons of the mixture and place it on the griddle. Sorta flatten the top out with your spatula or the back of a spoon. You want it to look like a little patty. Keep going until you have 4 or 5 patties going at a time. Cook each side until they are browned, nearly burnt, and crispy, about 3 minutes on each side. Do this in batches until you've used all the mixture. If the patties are sticking to the griddle, spray a little oil after each batch.

3 To bake: Crank up your oven to 425°F. Line a baking sheet with parchment paper. While the oven warms up, scoop up about 2 tablespoons of the mixture and place it on the lined baking sheet. Sorta flatten the top out with your spatula or back of the spoon. You want it to look like a little patty. Keep going until you run out of the quinoa mixture or space on the baking sheet. The fritters won't expand while they bake so you can really cram those fuckers in there if you want. Spray them with a little oil and bake, flipping halfway through, until both sides are browned and crispy, about 30 minutes total.

4 Serve warm or at room temperature.

CHEAT SHEET:

We love these with our 5-Minute Hummus (page 92), Tahini Cucumber Sauce (page 93), or Yellow Split Pea Dip (page 118). They're also great with our Herbed Flatbreads (page 128), or thrown on top of a salad or pasta that needs a little extra something.

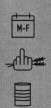

Makes about 15 to 18 fritters, depending on the size /
Cook time: 30 minutes on the stovetop, or 25 minutes in the oven

Tomato Chickpea Fritters

These fritters are a mash-up of a Greek salad and a chickpea burger that you never knew you needed.

1½ cups cooked chickpeas or 1 can (15 ounces), drained and rinsed

1 medium tomato, chopped

½ cup chopped green onions

2 tablespoons chopped parsley

1 tablespoon red wine vinegar

3 tablespoons ground flaxseeds, plus more as needed

¼ cup nutritional yeast (nooch), plus more as needed

½ teaspoon ground oregano

½ teaspoon garlic powder

½ teaspoon salt

2 tablespoons olive oil

Neutral oil for panfrying, such as like avocado, or spray olive oil for baking

1 Grab your food processor and throw in the chickpeas, tomato, green onions, parsley, and red wine vinegar. Pulse until everything is all minced up. Dump that mixture into a medium bowl and sprinkle the ground flaxseeds, nooch, oregano, garlic powder, and salt into the bowl. Then drizzle in the olive oil. Mix that shit up until everything kinda starts sticking together and there are no dry spots. If the mixture looks too wet, add more ground flaxseeds and nooch, 1 teaspoon at a time, until it thickens up.

2 To pan-fry: Warm up your griddle over medium-high heat. Scoop up about 2 tablespoons of the mixture and place it on the griddle in a pile. You want it to look like a cross between a patty and a pancake. Keep going until you have about 4 or 5 patties going at a time. Cook each side until it is browned, nearly burnt, and crispy, about 3 minutes each side. Do this in batches until you use up the mixture. If the patties are sticking to the griddle, spray a little oil onto the griddle as you go.

3 To bake: Crank up your oven to 425°F. Line a baking sheet with parchment paper. While the oven warms up, scoop up about 2 tablespoons of the mixture and place it on the baking sheet. Keep going until you run out of the chickpea mixture or space on the baking sheet. The fritters won't expand while they bake so you can really cram those fuckers in there. Spray them with a little oil then bake, flipping halfway through until both sides are browned and crispy, about 25 minutes. Serve warm or at room temperature.

TAHINI CUCUMBER
SAUCE (PAGE 93)

CHEAT SHEET:

We love these topped with chopped fresh tomatoes and herbs, our 5-Minute Hummus (page 92), Tahini Cucumber Sauce (page 93), Dill Buttermilk Dressing (page 89), or Yellow Split Pea Dip (page 118).

TOMATO CHICKPEA
FRITTERS (PAGE 144)

QUINOA ZUCCHINI
FRITTERS (PAGE 142)

SOMEWHERE BETWEEN QUESADILLA AND CALZONE

CHEAT SHEET:

These flatbreads pair great with our West Coast Chopped Salad (page 71) or our Everyday Cabbage Slaw (page 67). You can also cut them into slices and serve them with your favorite salsa as a great snack on your next movie night or for a laid-back dinner.

Summer Squash-Stuffed Flatbread

These stuffed flatbreads are sure to please even the pickiest of eaters. They're hearty, filling, and fucking beautiful up close. You can make the filling the night before and store it in the fridge until you're ready to assemble the flatbreads. If you don't have time to make the flatbread, just use your favorite brand of flour tortillas instead, but we recommend making them as written AT LEAST once because they really are something special.

Filling

1 tablespoon olive oil

1 yellow squash, grated (about 1 cup)

½ red onion, sliced

2 garlic cloves, minced

1 or 2 jalapeños, chopped, depending on your love of heat

1 tablespoon Braggs Liquid Aminos

1 teaspoon ground cumin

½ teaspoon ground coriander (or cumin, if you don't have it)

½ teaspoon chili powder

Grated zest of 1 lime

2 tablespoons chopped cilantro

½ cup 5-Minute Hummus (page 92)

Salt and black pepper

1½ cups of cooked black beans or 1 can (15 ounces), drained and rinsed

1 Warm up the olive oil in a large sauté pan over medium-high heat. Add the squash and onion and sauté until the onions start to soften and some of the liquid from the squash has evaporated, about 5 minutes. Toss in the garlic, jalapeños, and liquid aminos, and stir everything together. Now sprinkle in the cumin, coriander, chili powder, and lime zest. Cook for another minute, just to give the spices time to warm up. Turn off the heat and fold in the cilantro and hummus. Taste and add some salt and pepper or whatever the fuck you think it needs.

2 Grab a medium bowl and throw in the black beans. Smash the fuck out of them with a large spoon or potato masher until you see almost no whole beans. Scrape everything from the sauté pan into the bowl with the black beans, and stir until everything is well combined. Set this aside while you prepare the flatbread.

(recipe and ingredients continue)

Herbed Flatbread dough (page 128), completed up to step 4 and divided into 8 portions

Spray olive oil

House Crema (page 42), Cilantro Chimichurri (page 100), or your favorite salsa, for serving

3 When you're ready to stuff the flatbread, roll out each piece of flatbread dough on a well-floured surface into something close to the shape of a circle. Warm up your oven to 200°F.

4 We are going to stuff the flatbreads in the pan so have your filling nearby. Warm up a large sauté pan over medium-high heat and make sure it's nice and hot. Once it's hot, spray the pan lightly with oil, then place half of a rolled-out piece of dough right in and hold the other side up with your nondominant hand. Place 2 to 3 tablespoons of filling on the side of the flatbread that's touching the griddle, then stretch the piece you have in your hand over it to seal it together. It will kind of look like a stuffed quesadilla. Cook until the bottom looks golden brown, about 2 minutes, then flip that shit and continue cooking another 2 minutes. Once both sides are browned and some of the filling starts oozing out, you know you're good to go. Place the cooked, stuffed flatbread on a baking sheet and into the oven to stay warm while you make more. Keep going with these until you run out of dough.

5 Serve warm with some crema, chimichurri, or salsa.

Silky Zucchini Pasta with Fresh Tomato Salsa

Michelle has been cooking this summertime dinner for years and always called it "Green Noodles." It's a great way to use up cheap, in-season zucchini and delivers that creaminess you want from a pasta without being heavy. Now that you'll be cooking it for years, too, you can also call it "Green Noodles" or whatever. We thought we'd give it a real name since it's graduating to cookbook status.

1 pound spaghetti

Fresh Tomato Salsa (page 26; sub in dill for the green onions)

`Silky Zucchini Cream Sauce`

3 tablespoons olive oil

1 white onion, thinly sliced into ribbons

2 medium zucchini, grated on a box grater like cheese

Salt

3 garlic cloves, minced

Grated zest and juice of 1 lemon

1 cup nondairy milk

¼ cup chopped fresh dill

¼ cup chopped fresh parsley

¼ cup chopped fresh cilantro (or parsley if you're a hater)

2 tablespoons chopped fresh mint

1 Get the water boiling for the pasta as you make the cream sauce. Just follow the package directions for the noodles. They know their shit. Leave the pasta draining in the sink while you finish the rest of the dish.

2 While the water is coming to a boil is a great time to make the fresh tomato salsa if you haven't already. Remember to sub in dill for the green onions.

3 Make the zucchini cream sauce: Grab your largest skillet or braiser. You want the pan big enough for the shredded zucchini, and eventually the pasta, to have some room, so grab the biggest motherfucker you got. Warm up 2 tablespoons of the olive oil over medium heat. Add the onion and sauté until it starts to look a little translucent, 3 to 5 minutes. Add the shredded zucchini and a pinch of salt and cook this down until almost all the moisture that the zucchini releases is gone, 10 to 15 minutes. You barely have to pay attention here, just kinda stir the pan around every few minutes.

(recipe and ingredients continue)

2 tablespoons nutritional yeast (nooch)

1 tablespoon tahini

1 tablespoon ume plum vinegar (or more lemon juice with a pinch of salt)

2 teaspoons white or other mellow miso

Black pepper

4 When the zucchini looks almost ready, add the garlic and lemon zest and sauté for another minute or two. Remove from the heat and let it cool for a second. Grab your blender and add the lemon juice, milk, chopped herbs, nooch, tahini, the remaining 1 tablespoon olive oil, the plum vinegar, and miso. Scrape in the cooked zucchini mixture and run that shit until the sauce looks nice and smooth. Taste and add salt and pepper or whatever you think it needs.

5 Add the cooked pasta to the skillet, then drizzle over the cream sauce and toss. Serve warm or at room temperature with the fresh tomato salsa on top.

Red Lentils and Rice with Dill

Lentils: You know goddamn well you should eat more of them, but just the word "lentil" probably evokes some bland soup in your mind. This dish is a solid way to incorporate more lentils into your diet, especially since they disappear into the rice. Not to mention, it's so easy to prepare. What we're getting at is you're out of excuses.

2 tablespoons olive oil

1 red onion, chopped

Salt

1½ cups basmati rice, rinsed

1 tablespoon plus ¼ teaspoon no-salt yellow curry powder

1 cup red lentils, rinsed

3½ cups vegetable broth

3 cups chopped green beans

4 garlic cloves, minced

1 cup grated carrot

½ cup chopped fresh dill, plus more for garnish

¼ cup fresh lemon juice (about 2 lemons)

1 In a large pot, warm up 1 tablespoon of the olive oil over medium heat. Add half of the chopped red onion and a pinch of salt and sauté until the onion starts to look translucent, 3 to 5 minutes. Add the rice and 1 tablespoon of the curry powder and sauté until the rice is coated in the curry powder. Add the lentils and vegetable broth and bring the whole pot to a simmer. Once it's got a good simmer going, stir, then reduce the heat to low and throw on the lid. Let this cook until the rice is tender and all the water is absorbed, about 15 minutes.

2 While that shit is slowly cooking away, let's get going on the green beans. In a large braiser or sauté pan, heat the remaining 1 tablespoon oil over medium-high heat. Throw in the green beans and a pinch of salt and let 'em cook until they start to soften and get bright green, about 5 minutes. Add the rest of the chopped red onion and keep cooking until the green beans are tender but not mushy, another 5 to 7 minutes. If the pan starts looking too dry before the beans are cooked to your liking, just add a tablespoon or two of water. No big deal. Once they look good to you, add the garlic and remaining ¼ teaspoon curry powder and sauté for 1 minute more before removing from the heat.

3 By now the rice should be done and most of the lentils will have disappeared into it. That's perfect. Add ½ teaspoon salt and fluff the rice mixture up with a fork to get it all mixed in. Fold in the grated carrot, cooked green beans, and dill. Drizzle with the lemon juice and mix one more time.

4 Serve warm or at room temperature with extra dill on top for looks.

Sesame Noodles with Pan-Seared Tofu

Michelle has been making some version of this dish once a month for twenty years. It's so fucking versatile. Add roasted cauliflower (see Sheet Pan Cauliflower, page 102) or broccoli to the side instead of cucumbers. Toss shredded carrots or frozen edamame into the pasta water just before draining it. Replace the tahini with peanut butter. The options go on forever.

1 pound udon noodles or similar-style pasta

Sesame Sauce

3 tablespoons rice vinegar

2 tablespoons tahini or similar sesame paste

1 tablespoon tamari or soy sauce

1 tablespoon toasted sesame oil

2 garlic cloves, grated

2 teaspoons grated fresh ginger

2 teaspoons chili-garlic sauce or similar-style sauce

For Serving

Pan-seared tofu*

Cucumbers sticks

Chopped fresh herbs, such as basil, mint, cilantro, or green onion

Toasted sesame seeds

*Make the pan-seared torn tofu from the Banh Mi–Inspired Sammie (page 64).

1 Cook your noodles according to the package directions because they know their shit. Right before you drain them, pull out 3 tablespoons of the warm, starchy water from the pot and set it aside.

2 Make the sesame sauce: In a large bowl, whisk together the reserved starchy water, the vinegar, tahini, tamari, sesame oil, garlic, ginger, and chili-garlic paste. Toss the warm noodles into the bowl and stir until everything is coated.

3 To serve: Add a pile of sesame noodles to each plate, top with a serving of tofu, a side of cucumber sticks, and garnish with whatever herbs you like and some toasted sesame seeds.

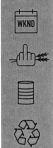

Makes about 6 cups / Cook time: a couple hours, mostly inactive

Sunday Beans

Sunday beans are more of a lifestyle than a recipe. They don't require lots of attention, but they do need some time to do their thing. So while you're at home on a Sunday, doing the boring shit that being alive requires, simmer a pot of beans on the stove. You'll cook enough to eat and use in your recipes for the week. Cooking time will vary based on what beans you're using and how long you've soaked them, but you'll be able to handle it. We swear.

1 pound dried beans

1 tablespoon olive oil

1 onion, chopped

1 carrot, chopped

1 celery ribs, chopped

3 garlic cloves, crushed with the broad side of your knife

1 dried chipotle pepper (optional)

Salt and black pepper

1 Pour your beans into a colander and rinse, discarding any with cracks. Throw them in a large bowl and add water to cover by 2 inches. Let them soak there for a couple hours. Do this in the morning while you make your coffee, tea, or whatever your little ritual is. No time to soak? That's fine, just know that it's gonna take longer to cook them.

2 When you are ready to cook, add the olive oil to a large soup pot with a lid over medium-high heat. Add the onion, carrot, and celery and cook until everything has softened up, 8 to 10 minutes. Stir in the garlic and chipotle pepper (if using). Pour in the beans and their soaking liquid and add enough water to cover them by at least 3 inches. Bring to a boil over high heat for 10 minutes, stirring frequently. Reduce the heat to medium-low, cover, and let this pot simmer until the beans are tender, 1 to 3 hours. If you start running out of water while you're cooking, just add a cup or two of warm water to the pot and keep simmering.

3 When they beans are *almost* tender, add salt to the pot, ½ teaspoon at a time until it tastes good to you. Adding salt too early in the cooking process can make the beans tough, so waiting has its rewards. When the beans are done, taste and add some black pepper or more salt, if needed. You can scoop the cooked beans into recipes, puree them right in the pot, or do whatever the fuck you want. They're your beans.

FIELD GUIDE:
BEAN COUNTER

We call for a lot of different kinds of beans in this book, so we thought it was only fair to include a handy guide to all the different ways you can get 1 cup of them. Obviously, it's always more affordable to cook the beans yourself, but when time is at a minimum, canned beans are major lifesavers. Whether you are cooking them at home or using a can, here's the math to use so that you don't have to spend your afternoon counting beans.

1 POUND DRIED BEANS   2 CUPS DRIED BEANS   6 CUPS COOKED BEANS

1 CUP DRIED BEANS   3 CUPS COOKED BEANS

1 (15-OUNCE) CAN BEANS, DRAINED   1½ CUPS COOKED BEANS

1 POUND DRIED BEANS   4 CANS OF BEANS

Torn Tofu Satay with Sunflower Butter Sauce

You have every right to be skeptical of grilled tofu. BUT since you're holding our book in your hands, that's a big sign of trust, right? We would never do you (or ourselves) dirty like that. We've been victims of some apathetic tofu dishes before, no love, no seasoning, and that shit has to stop. Bad tofu comes from bad or lazy cooks, always. Doubting yourself? Stop. This dish is so packed with flavor that it's gonna turn tofu around for the nonbelievers.

1 package (14 ounces) extra-firm tofu

½ teaspoon salt

Peanut or other high-heat neutral oil, for greasing the grill

Marinade

1 cup full-fat coconut milk

2 tablespoons tamari or soy sauce

2 tablespoons no-salt yellow curry power

1 tablespoon chili-garlic sauce or similar-style hot sauce

Juice of 1 lime

Sunflower Butter Sauce

½ cup coconut milk

¼ cup sunflower, peanut, or almond butter

3 tablespoons rice vinegar

1 tablespoon soy sauce or tamari

1 tablespoon minced fresh ginger

1 Grab a pack of long skewers and set them aside in some water to prepare them for grilling.

2 Drain the tofu, press it, and then rip it up into bite-size pieces about the size of an ice cube (see page 66 to learn more about tearing tofu by hand). You want each cube to be big enough so that it stays on the skewer but not so big that it's awkward as fuck to eat. Stick the tofu in a small pot with the salt and add enough water to cover it. Bring to a boil over medium-high heat and cook for 10 minutes. This helps improve the texture of the tofu and gives it some flavor before it sits in the marinade.

3 While the tofu is boiling, make the marinade: In a large glass, mix the coconut milk, soy sauce, curry powder, chili-garlic sauce, and lime juice until there are no clumps. Set this aside.

4 When the tofu is done, drain it, and when it's cool enough to handle, stick the tofu on the skewers. Just remember to leave at least 1 inch on either end so you can move the

(recipe and ingredients continue)

1 shallot or ¼ onion, chopped

Juice of 1 lime

For the Wraps

Butter lettuce or green leaf lettuce

Cucumbers

Carrots

Green onions

Mint

Chopped peanuts

Lime wedges

skewers easily. Generously brush the tofu with the marinade on all sides and let that shit chill while you make the dipping sauce.

5 Make the dipping sauce: Throw the coconut milk into a blender or food processor with the sunflower butter, vinegar, soy sauce, ginger, shallot, and lime juice. Run that shit until it's smooth. The dipping sauce is done, done, done. You can let this shit sit overnight in the fridge or for a couple hours, if you're trying to get your prep out of the way, but it's ready to go whenever you are, no wait necessary.

6 When it's time, grab your grill or grill pan. Get that shit hot, around 500°F, and greased up. Place the skewers right on there and brush with some more marinade as they cook. Turn them after 4 to 5 minutes or whenever you get some nice, deep grill marks. Brush them again as you turn them to make sure they absorb lots of fucking flavor. Try to get some grill marks on as many sides as possible without knocking any tofu off the skewers. You almost want to char them like a roasted bell pepper. The tofu will be better for it, we swear. This whole process should take around 10 minutes.

7 When the tofu is done, brush it with whatever marinade you have left and let it sit for a minute or two to cool down.

8 Serve warm or at room temperature with the sunflower butter sauce for dipping. To make this more of a meal, serve the skewers alongside some lettuce leaves and make lettuce wraps out of them. Cut some cucumber, carrots, green onions, and mint into slices so that they'll fit inside the lettuce leaves, with some chopped peanuts on the side for some extra crunch. Drizzle with the dipping sauce and finish with a squeeze of fresh lime. Chomp, chomp, bitch. You're eating in style now.

Dirty Rice with Lentils

Dirty rice is a Southern staple that we've reimagined with lentils. It has all the nostalgia of the old dish without all the random animal bits. It's a meal unto itself, but pair it up with our Braised Greens (page 125) and Morning Cornbread (page 28) for a full spread.

1 tablespoon olive oil or nondairy butter

½ white onion, diced

Salt

1 green bell pepper, diced

1 red bell pepper, diced

2 celery ribs, diced

1½ teaspoons dried thyme

1 teaspoon paprika

½ teaspoon smoked paprika

Black pepper

3 garlic cloves, minced

1 tablespoon tomato paste

2 cups long-grain brown rice

1 tablespoon Bragg Liquid Aminos or soy sauce

½ cup black lentils

2 bay leaves

5 cups water or vegetable broth

For Serving

Sliced green onion or chopped fresh parsley

Lemon wedges

1 In a large soup pot with a lid, warm up the oil over medium-high heat. Add the onion and a pinch of salt and sauté until the onion starts to brown, about 8 minutes. Add both bell peppers and the celery and cook until the peppers start to soften, another 4 to 5 minutes. Sprinkle in the thyme, paprika, smoked paprika, and ¼ teaspoon black pepper and cook for a minute, until your kitchen really starts smelling good. Add the garlic and tomato paste and cook for another minute while you spread around the tomato paste.

2 Stir in the rice, liquid aminos, lentils, and bay leaves. Add the water and bring this to a simmer. Reduce the heat to low, throw on the lid, and cook for 30 minutes. Start checking to see if the rice and lentils are tender. Still not done, but the water level is looking low? Add another 1 cup water to the pot and throw on the lid to cook for another 5 to 10 minutes. When the rice and lentils are tender, fluff the whole pot with a fork, then taste. Add more salt or whatever kind of seasoning you want.

3 To serve: Top each plate with some sliced green onions or parsley with a lemon wedge on the side and some black pepper on top.

FIELD GUIDE:
BUILD A BURRITO BAR

You might not have noticed, but this book contains everything you need to make a killer burrito bar for your next gathering. You'll need the following dishes and ingredients:

- WARM FLOUR TORTILLAS

- RED PEPPER RICE (PAGE 110), CILANTRO RICE (PAGE 116), OR CUMIN RICE (PAGE 115)

- SUNDAY BEANS (PAGE 155)

- GRILLED TOMATILLO AND AVOCADO SALSA (PAGE 108) OR FRESH TOMATO SALSA (PAGE 26)

- QUESO BLANCO (PAGE 96)

- SHREDDED LETTUCE OR CABBAGE OR EVERYDAY CABBAGE SLAW (PAGE 67)

- CHOPPED TOMATOES

- SLICED AVOCADO

You'll have enough for several burritos for a crowd of 1 to 6 people, depending on how hungry you all are. Make all the dishes over the course of 2 days to spread out the work. When your guests arrive, you won't have to do anything more than point them to the spread and relax while they overfill their plates.

Place all of these dishes in the order you think people should use them to build their burritos. You can warm the tortillas and put them on the table first. Next come the beans and rice, salsa, and queso. Set your fresh ingredients like lettuce, tomatoes, and avocado at the end of the table. You can't help it if your guests go out of order, but at least you'll know you tried to set them up for success.

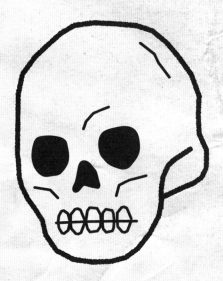

GRILLED TOMATILLO AND
AVOCADO SALSA (PAGE 108)

RED PEPPER RICE
(PAGE 110)

POBLANO HOME FRIES
(PAGE 38)

EVERYDAY CABBAGE SLAW
(PAGE 67)

SUNDAY BEANS
(PAGE 155)

Makes enough for 4 people / Cook time: 40 minutes

Baked Butternut Squash with Tomato Lentil Sauce

This is a take on an unforgettable dish Michelle used to have as a kid at a local Afghani restaurant. The butternut squash just melts in your mouth. The seemingly simply tomato lentil sauce brings depth to the flavor, and the yogurt perfectly ties the whole thing together. Make it once and you will be obsessed. It's a fucking promise. We love this dish as is, but the leftovers are fantastic thrown into a Savory Breakfast Hand Pie (page 30). You'll see.

Baked Butternut Squash

1 large butternut squash

2 tablespoons olive oil

¼ cup cane sugar

½ teaspoon ground cinnamon

½ teaspoon ground coriander

¼ teaspoon salt

¼ cup veggie broth or water

Tomato Lentil Sauce

1 tablespoon olive oil

1 yellow onion, chopped

Salt

2 teaspoons ground coriander

1 teaspoon black pepper

½ teaspoon ground turmeric

3 garlic cloves, minced

1½ cups tomato sauce

1 cup veggie broth or water

1½ cups cooked black lentils

1 tablespoon ume plum vinegar or large pinch of salt

1 Make the butternut squash: Warm up your oven to 350°F. Grab a large baking dish with a cover (or a piece of foil large enough to cover the baking dish) and set it to the side.

2 Peel the squash with your veggie peeler. Cut your butternut squash in half crosswise right off the bat to make that shit easier to handle. Now cut each chunk in half, scraping out the seeds. You should end up with 8 good-size pieces. Grab a large bowl and toss them in the oil, then sprinkle with the sugar, cinnamon, coriander, and salt. Dump all of that in the large baking dish you set aside, pour in the veggie broth, cover, and throw it in the oven until the squash is fork-tender, 30 to 40 minutes. You know, easy to stab with a fork.

3 While that's baking, make the tomato lentil sauce: Grab a large sauté pan or skillet, warm it up over medium-high heat, and add the olive oil. Throw in the onion and a small pinch of salt and cook until the onion starts to brown in some spots, 8 to 10 minutes. Add the coriander, black pepper, and turmeric and cook for another minute so that

(recipe and ingredients continue)

**Garlic-Mint Yogurt
(page 94)**

Fresh mint

all those spices get a chance to warm up. Stir in the garlic, tomato sauce, and veggie broth so that everything is mixed up, then fold in the lentils and the plum vinegar. Reduce the heat to medium-low and cook all of this together for 10 minutes, adding more broth if the sauce starts looking too thick.

4 To serve: Ladle some of the tomato lentil sauce and garlic-mint yogurt into the bottom of a plate or bowl, place a piece of the roasted butternut squash on top, then add more tomato lentil mixture and yogurt on top. Garnish with little pieces of fresh mint, if you are feeling fancy.

CHEAT SHEET:

This goes great with a side of Cumin Rice (page 115), Braised Greens (page 125), and Herbed Flatbreads (page 128).

FIELD GUIDE:
THE WHOLE ENCHILADA

Enchiladas (especially our Green Enchiladas on page 171) are an easy way to get dinner on the table and get everyone stoked as hell. Plus, you can freeze a tray of unbaked enchiladas, cook them as you normally would, and boom, super-easy homemade meal. Below are some different enchilada filling options from this book so that you can keep the meals going with the skills and recipes you already have. Follow our recipe for Green Enchiladas (page 171) for the sauce and the assembly and baking instructions. You'll get the hang of it in no time. You might want to cover the thawed tray with some fresh salsa to brighten up their look when they come out of the oven.

SUMMER SQUASH ENCHILADAS:
ONE BATCH OF FILLING FROM THE SUMMER SQUASH-STUFFED FLATBREAD (PAGE 147)

NOSTALGIA ENCHILADAS:
ONE BATCH OF CHEATER BEANS (PAGE 138) AND ONE BATCH OF RED PEPPER RICE (PAGE 110)

BEAN AND CHEESE ENCHILADAS:
HALF BATCH OF SUNDAY BEANS (PAGE 155) AND ONE BATCH OF QUESO BLANCO (PAGE 96)

CHEAT SHEET:

These will last for up to 5 days in the fridge. You can freeze a whole tray if you're feeling on top of your shit, and they'll be good for 3 months in there. Thaw them in your fridge overnight before warming them up in the oven at 350°F for 15 to 20 minutes.

Green Enchiladas

Enchiladas are universally loved, and this recipe is no exception. You could wake anyone from a dead sleep and offer them a warm enchilada and they'd chow down. Every. Single. Time.

Filling

1 tablespoon olive oil

½ white onion, chopped

1 red bell pepper, chopped

1 can (20 ounces) young jackfruit,* drained, rinsed, and chopped

2 teaspoons ground cumin

2 teaspoons smoked paprika

1 teaspoon chili powder

1 tablespoon Bragg Liquid Aminos

2 garlic cloves, minced

1 cup corn kernels, fresh or frozen

1 cup Queso Blanco (page 96)

Enchiladas

Grilled Tomatillo and Avocado Salsa (page 108)

12 corn tortillas

½ cup Queso Blanco (page 96)

For Serving

Chopped fresh cilantro

Hot sauce

Sliced jalapeños

Minced red onion

*Don't know shit about jackfruit? Learn how to buy and prep it the Field Guide on page 81.

1 Warm up your oven to 375°F.

2 Make the filling: Warm the oil over medium heat in a large sauté pan or skillet with a lid. Add the onion and sauté that shit 'til it starts to get a little golden, about 6 minutes. Add the bell pepper and cook until it starts to soften, another 5 minutes. Add the jackfruit and sprinkle with the cumin, smoked paprika, chili powder, liquid aminos, and garlic. Cook for 2 minutes so that everything can get mixed together. Toss in the corn and the queso blanco and keep cooking just until everything is warm, about another minute. Remove from the heat.

3 Now you're finally gonna make the enchiladas: Grab a rectangular baking dish no bigger than 9 × 13 inches. Cover the bottom of the dish with about 1½ cups of the salsa. Using a griddle, your oven, or the microwave, warm up the tortillas. Kinda dip the tortilla around in the salsa so that the bottom side is all coated. Fill it with a couple spoonfuls of filling and then roll it up so that it sits seam-side down in the dish. You know how enchiladas are supposed to look, so trust yourself. Keep going until you run out of space or out of filling. Pour the remaining ½ cup salsa over the enchiladas and drizzle the queso blanco on top.

4 Cover the dish tightly with foil and throw it in the oven for 20 minutes. Take off the foil and cook it for 5 more. Let it cool for a minute or two before serving.

5 To serve: Feel free to top those gorgeous enchiladas with cilantro, hot sauce, sliced jalapeños, or minced red onion.

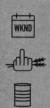

Makes enough for 4 people / Cook time: 2½ hours, plus bean soaking time, mostly inactive

El Congrí de Flor

Congrí, the Cuban staple of red beans and rice, might be known worldwide, but every single family makes theirs just a lil' bit different. And what part of the island your family is from usually dictates whether you grew up eating this dish with black beans instead of red beans. Michelle's wife, Kyria, grew up eating her Grandma Flor's version of the iconic meal, which included red beans. When Flor passed away, the recipe was lost and all that was left were memories of the comfort food classic. After much trial and error, this is the recipe that brought back all the nostalgia for Kyria. We all now eat it at least once a month, and we're bringing this dish from Flor's kitchen to yours.

1 cup dried red beans

2 bay leaves

Salt

2 tablespoons olive oil, plus more for drizzling

1 medium onion, finely chopped

1 red or green bell pepper, finely chopped

2 canned chipotle peppers in adobo sauce, seeded and finely chopped

5 garlic cloves, minced

1 tablespoon smoked paprika

2 teaspoons dried oregano

2 teaspoons ground cumin

½ cup dry white wine or vegetable broth

2 cups long-grain white rice, such as basmati, rinsed

Lime juice

½ cup chopped fresh cilantro

1 Rinse the beans, picking out any that look fucked up, then put them in a saucepan and add water to cover them by at least 3 inches. Let these soak overnight or for a few hours to reduce your cooking time.

2 When it's time to get going, do not change the water. Just set the pan over high heat and throw in the bay leaves. Let this shit come to a boil for 10 minutes, then reduce the heat to medium and let the pot simmer until the beans are soft, about 1½ hours. If it's starting to look like there's less than an inch of water above the beans, pour a lil' more warm water in. Right before the beans are done, add ½ teaspoon salt to the pot. If you add that shit too soon, it can make the beans cook slower or worse, never soften.

3 When the beans are about done, warm up the olive oil in a large pot over medium-high heat and add the onion. Reduce the heat to medium-low and cook, stirring occasionally, until slightly browned, 5 to 7 minutes. Add the bell pepper, chipotle peppers, garlic, smoked paprika, oregano, cumin, and ½ teaspoon salt and cook, stirring often, until everything is soft and your kitchen smells amazing, 6 to 9 minutes.

Chopped fresh cilantro
Lime wedges
Sliced bananas

4 Add the wine and use it to scrape off any burnt-on flavor that might have stuck to the bottom of the pot. That's flavor concentrate—you're gonna wanna use that. Add the rice and cook it all together for about 1 minute so that the rice gets coated.

5 Add the beans and their cooking liquid to the pot of rice. You want about 3 cups of liquid in there, so if there wasn't enough bean broth, add more vegetable broth to make up the difference. Bring all this to a boil over medium-high heat, cover, and reduce the heat to maintain a gentle, low simmer. Cook until the water is absorbed and the rice is tender, about 18 minutes. Don't peek in the pot while this is going on; just set a timer for 15 minutes and only start checking after it goes off. Taste and season with salt and lime juice to get it however you like.

6 Just before serving, stir in the cilantro and drizzle with a lil' bit of olive oil.

7 To serve: Serve warm with extra cilantro on top and lime wedges on the side. To be just like Flor, throw a sliced banana on the side. Trust Grandma. It works.

CHEAT SHEET:

This also goes great with our Everyday Cabbage Slaw (page 67), Grilled Plantains (page 99), and Cilantro Chimichurri Sauce (page 100).

EVERYDAY CABBAGE SLAW
(PAGE 67)

EL CONGRÍ DE FLOR
(PAGE 172)

GRILLED PLANTAINS
(PAGE 99)

CILANTRO CHIMICHURRI
(PAGE 100)

CHEAT SHEET:

To round out your meal, pair this mac and cheese with a side of our Braised Greens (page 125) or just toss some roasted broccoli right into the noodle dish. Make sure you add a little green to your meal, k? A fully beige dinner is never okay.

White Mac and Cheese

The sauce here is a trimmed-down version of our Queso Blanco (page 96), but we loved it so much we thought it deserved its own page. This mac and cheese is a great place to sneak some bonus veggies, like roasted broccoli or even peas, in with the pasta. We've given you the base, now go play around with this shit and make it your own.

All-Purpose White Cream Sauce

1 tablespoon olive oil

1 shallot or ¼ onion, chopped

2 russet potatoes, peeled and chopped

1 cup vegetable broth

1½ cups nondairy milk

⅓ cup nutritional yeast (nooch)

2 tablespoons cashew butter*

1 tablespoon Bragg Liquid Aminos or tamari

1 tablespoon ume plum vinegar or ½ teaspoon salt

2 tablespoons fresh lemon juice

¼ teaspoon ground nutmeg

For Serving

1 pound pasta, like shells or cavatelli, cooked according to the package instructions

Onion Croutons (optional; page 58)

*Not sure about cashew butter? See our Cheat Sheet on page 97 for an alternative.

1 Make the all-purpose white cream sauce: In a large sauté pan or skillet with a lid, warm up the olive oil over medium heat. Add the shallot and sauté it around until it gets some color, about 5 minutes. Add the chopped potato and stir until it's all mixed up with the shallot, then pour in the veggie broth. Cover the pan and let it simmer away until the potatoes are tender enough to easily push a fork through them, about 10 minutes. Let them cool in the pan for a few minutes while you get the rest of the shit ready.

2 Pour the milk, nooch, cashew butter, liquid aminos, plum vinegar, lemon juice, and nutmeg into your blender. Add the cooked potatoes and whatever broth is still left in the pan to the blender, then let that shit run. To really make a silky sauce, you want to run that shit for at least 30 seconds to 1 minute, depending on the strength of your blender. Taste it and if the texture is still a little grainy, keep blending because this shit should be smooth as hell.

3 To serve: Add the cooked pasta to a large serving pan or bowl and pour the white cheese sauce over top. Stir until everything is coated. Serve as is or top with a handful of our Onion Croutons for a little crunch.

Makes about 32 balls, enough for 6 to 8 people /
Cook time: 1 hour 15 minutes

Eggplant Polpetti

When you're cooking for this yourself, they're meatballs. When you're cooking to impress, they're polpetti. But no matter the name, you're gonna want to make these at least once a month for the rest of your life.

1 tablespoon olive oil

1 shallot or ¼ onion, chopped

1 large eggplant, chopped (about 5½ cups)

1 tablespoon fennel seeds, chopped

1 tablespoon chopped fresh rosemary

1 tablespoon Bragg Liquid Aminos

1½ cups cooked kidney beans or 1 can (15 ounces), drained and rinsed

4 garlic cloves

2 tablespoons minced fresh parsley

1 teaspoon smoked paprika

½ teaspoon black pepper

½ teaspoon salt

3 tablespoons nutritional yeast (nooch)

1¼ cups bread crumbs, finely ground and dried, homemade or store-bought

Spray oil

1 Warm up the olive oil over medium heat in your largest skillet. Throw the shallot in and let it cook for a minute. Add the eggplant and toss it around to coat it with the oil. Cook this until the eggplant begins to brown and soften, 6 to 8 minutes. Now let's add some flavor and throw in the fennel seeds and rosemary. Drizzle the liquid aminos over the top and let this whole thing cook together for a minute or two more. Remove from the heat.

2 Once the eggplant has cooled a little, grab your food processor. Add everything from the eggplant pan, the kidney beans, garlic, parsley, smoked paprika, black pepper, and salt. Run that shit until it looks smooth. Scrape the mixture out into a bowl and fold in the nutritional yeast and bread crumbs. Mix everything up until it looks nice and uniform.

3 Warm up your oven to 375°F. Line a baking sheet with parchment paper.

4 It's time to ball. Grab some of the eggplant mixture, roll it into a ball about the size of a Ping-Pong ball and put it on the baking sheet. If your mixture feels a little too wet, add some more bread crumbs, a tablespoon at a time, until it holds together. Too dry? Do that same shit with water. No matter what, keep going until you run out of eggplant mixture.

5 Spray the top of the balls with some oil and stick the pan in the oven until the bottom of the balls get nice and browned, about 30 minutes. Serve warm.

CHEAT SHEET:

We like our Eggplant Polpetti drowned in a few cups of 30-Minute Marinara (page 139) with a side of crostini, or on top of a pile of bucatini. For a fast and filling homemade meal, freeze the polpetti in one layer, then transfer them to an airtight container or bag. Store in the freezer for up to 3 months. When you're ready to reheat them, warm up your oven to 350°F and spray a baking dish with a little oil. Add the polpetti. Cover with foil and bake for 15 to 20 minutes until warm.

Makes enough for 4 to 6 people / Cook time: 2 hours

Pumpkin Lasagna Rolls

Some of the best things in life are rolled. Tacos. Sushi. Weed.
Cinnamon rolls. So why not lasagna?

1 box (1 pound) lasagna
noodles, cooked according
to the package directions

All-Purpose White Cream
Sauce (see White Mac
and Cheese, page 177),
completed up to step 2

2 cups pumpkin or butternut
squash puree, canned or
homemade (see page 47)

Extra-Creamy Tofu
Ricotta

1 block (14 ounces) extra-
firm tofu

1 tablespoon olive oil

1 tablespoon ume plum
vinegar

Juice of ½ lemon (about
1 tablespoon)

4 garlic cloves, minced

2 tablespoons nutritional
yeast (nooch)

½ cup All-Purpose White
Cream Sauce

For Assembly and
Serving

Fresh sage leaves

Panko Pasta Topping
(page 98)

1 Warm up your oven to 375°F and grab a large baking dish,
the one you'll use to make the lasagna. Lay out the cooked
lasagna noodles on a large baking sheet in strips so that
they'll be easier to roll later.

2 Make the ricotta: Take the tofu out of the package and
squeeze out as much water as you can. Crush the tofu into
a medium bowl with your hands, squeezing it through your
fingers so that you get a sorta cottage cheese texture.
There's no wrong way to do this shit. Just make sure the tofu
is in small crumbles. Pour in the olive oil, plum vinegar, and
lemon juice. Toss, then add the garlic, nooch, and the ½ cup
of the cream sauce. Mix until totally combined.

3 Now it's time to roll: Pour 1½ cups of the white cream
sauce on the bottom of the baking dish you set aside so
that the noodles don't stick. Spread 2 to 3 tablespoons of
the pumpkin puree onto a lasagna noodle, leaving ½ inch
from either of the short ends empty. Dollop 2 to 3 spoonfuls
of the ricotta, no more than 3 tablespoons, over the puree
on the noodle and then, starting from a short end, roll the
noodle like you are rolling up a sleeping bag. Place the
stuffed noodle into the prepared baking dish however you
want, seam side down. Keep rolling until you run out of
noodles. When you're done, pour the remaining white sauce
over the rolled-up noodles. Place some fresh sage leaves on
top of the sauce-covered rolled noodles.

4 Cover the tray with foil and bake for 20 minutes. Then
take off the foil and bake until the edges start to look golden
brown, about 20 more minutes. Let this cool for 10 minutes
and top with panko pasta topping before serving.

CHEAT SHEET:

Serve these roll-ups alongside our Simple Side
Salad with House Vinaigrette (page 50) or Braised
Greens (page 125). If you want to turn this dish
into a make-ahead meal, prepare it in a freezer-
friendly tray and then stop after you've complete
assembled the dish. To reheat, bake at 375°F,
covered with foil, for 30 minutes, then remove th
foil and bake for an additional 20 minutes.

Swee

Noth

Cookies, Cakes, and Your Favorite Desserts

...et ...ings

Brown Sugar Cookies

These are somewhere between a standard sugar cookie and a snickerdoodle, a delicious spot to be in. We've included two ways of using the dough because life's too short to have cookies that can do only one thing. Your dessert should work as hard as you.

2¼ cups all-purpose flour

½ teaspoon baking soda

¼ teaspoon salt

¼ teaspoon ground cinnamon

2 tablespoons ground golden flaxseeds*

2 tablespoons nondairy milk

½ cup nondairy butter, softened

¾ cup brown sugar

Turbinado or more brown sugar for sprinkling (optional)

*We like golden flaxseeds here because they disappear better into the final cookie. If you can't find them, just use regular ground flaxseeds. The little flecks of brown look cute, too.

1 In a medium bowl, whisk together the flour, baking soda, salt, and ground cinnamon. In a small glass, whisk together the flaxseeds and nondairy milk. Set all this shit aside.

2 With your stand mixer fitted with the paddle attachment, beat the butter and brown sugar together until they look fluffy, almost like whipped cream. You can do this by hand with a big-ass spoon and your strongest arm, too. It will just take longer. Pour in the flax mixture and beat until it's all combined. Lastly, add the flour mixture and beat it into the butter mixture at low speed until there aren't any dry spots. The hardest part is over. Stick this in the fridge to chill for at least an hour or up to 3 days.

3 When you're ready to make the cookies, warm up your oven to 375°F and line two baking sheets with parchment paper. You can either roll out the dough and make sugar cookie cutouts or grab off the dough into little balls for drop cookies. Your call.

4 To make sugar cookie cutouts: Place a piece of parchment paper on your counter and sprinkle it with some flour to prevent your dough from sticking. Place the chilled dough on the parchment, sprinkle some flour onto the dough, then cover the whole thing with another sheet of parchment. Roll the dough between the parchment until it is ¼ inch thick. Peel off the top layer of parchment, then cut out shapes using your favorite cookie cutters. If you want, sprinkle the tops with sugar for looks. Place the cookies on the prepared baking sheets and bake until the edges look firm and the bottoms are golden brown, 10 to 12 minutes.

5 To make drop cookies: Grab a golf-ball-sized amount of dough and roll it into a ball. Place on the prepared baking sheets and keep going until you run out of dough. Press each ball down until the top is flat and sprinkle it with sugar. Bake until the edges are firm and the bottom of the cookies are starting to brown, about 12 minutes.

6 When the cookies are done, leave them on the baking sheets for a few minutes, then transfer them to a cooling rack to cool completely.

Rosemary Pecan Scones with Maple Glaze

We take issue with most scone recipes because they're too fucking sweet. If we wanted to just freebase sugar, we would have grabbed some strawberry candy straws from the market. If we're baking, we want classy, complex flavors, baby. The rosemary in these adds a depth you won't find in most scones and cuts down on the sweetness, letting the maple glaze deliver those autumnal vibes you crave year-round.

Scones

1 cup almond milk

1 tablespoon fresh lemon juice

3 cups all-purpose flour or whole wheat pastry flour

2 tablespoons baking powder

3 tablespoons cane or turbinado sugar, plus more for sprinkling

¼ teaspoon salt

¼ cup cold coconut oil

2 tablespoons cold nondairy butter

2 tablespoons olive oil

1 tablespoon chopped fresh rosemary

¾ cup chopped pecans

Grapeseed oil, olive oil, or almond milk for brushing

1 Crank the oven to 425°F. Line a baking sheet with parchment paper or foil.

2 Make the scones: In a small cup, combine the milk and lemon juice and let it sit. In a large bowl, mix together the flour, baking powder, cane sugar, and salt. Cut the coconut oil and nondairy butter into the flour using your hands or a fork until it all looks kind of grainy and there are no large chunks left. Just smash it around for a while and you'll be fine. Drizzle in the olive oil and mix it up so that the oil's not forming a glob in the flour somewhere.

3 Make a well in the center of the flour and pour in the milk mixture and the chopped rosemary. Mix it together until it is almost all the way combined but stop short. You still gotta add the nuts. Fold in the pecans but be careful not to overmix. You don't want dense scones. Shape the dough into a ball in the bowl using your hands and then move it to your cutting board.

4 Pat down the dough into a round no more than 1½ inches high. Take a sharp knife and cut that fucker up into 8 to 10 wedges like a pizza. Pull out and place each little wedge on your prepared baking sheet.

Maple Glaze

1 tablespoon nondairy butter

1 sprig of fresh rosemary

¼ cup maple syrup

⅓ cup powdered sugar

5 Brush the outsides of the scones with a little grapeseed oil, olive oil, or almond milk; sprinkle a little cane sugar on for looks; and then stick that shit in the oven until the bottoms start to brown, 12 to 15 minutes.

6 While the scones are baking, make the glaze: In your smallest saucepan over low heat, melt the butter, then throw in the rosemary sprig and maple syrup. Bring this up to a simmer, stir, then remove from the heat. We just wanna infuse that syrup with all that rosemary flavor, so let this sit for however long you've got. When you're ready to glaze, pull out the rosemary sprig and whisk in the powdered sugar until it's all incorporated and no chunks remain.

7 When the scones are done, let them cool on a cooling rack for 10 to 15 minutes before glazing. If you do it while they're still hot, the scones will just absorb the glaze and it won't look like you did anything. Drizzle the glaze over with a whisk or a fork and draw little lines all over. Now go enjoy that shit.

FUCK YEAH EH!

Makes enough for 6 to 8 people to munch on / Cook time: 25 minutes, mostly inactive

Coconut Caramel Corn

Consider this a tool in your tool chest of "fancy" recipes. It's simple as shit, affordable, and everyone loves it. Any idiot can make popcorn but only YOU can make homemade caramel corn. And when everyone's raving about it, you'll just casually be like, "Oh this ol' thing?" while you flip your hair.

8 cups unseasoned popped popcorn*

¼ cup refined coconut oil or nondairy butter

½ cup brown sugar

¼ cup maple syrup

½ teaspoon salt

½ teaspoon baking soda

½ cup shredded unsweetened coconut

½ cup finely chopped nuts, such as toasted peanuts or cashews

*Yes, you can buy pre-popped popcorn, but you should just do this shit yourself on the stovetop. It's not fucking hard. We've got instructions after this recipe if you still feel overwhelmed.

1 Warm up your oven to 250°F and line a rimmed baking sheet with parchment paper.

2 Pour the popcorn into one big bowl with tall sides or two medium bowls so that it doesn't spill out later when you're trying to mix it. You'll know if your bowl is too small. Don't try to make it work. You'll just get mad and take it out on the popcorn.

3 Make the caramel: In a small saucepan over medium heat, melt the coconut oil. When it's totally melted, add the brown sugar, maple syrup, and salt. Simmer that shit for 2½ to 3 minutes, whisking constantly so nothing burns. You want the sugar crystals to dissolve and a constant stream of bubbles to roll through the whole sauce. You'll know the sugar has dissolved when you can't feel the grains while you whisk.

4 Stir in the baking soda and turn off the heat. The mixture will kinda bubble up and turn less see-through. Mix it up well and pour it over the popcorn. Stir and stir until all that shit is lightly coated in that caramel. Sprinkle in the shredded coconut and chopped nuts, and stir again until everything looks nice and coated.

5 Pour the popcorn mixture on the lined baking sheet in an evenish layer, turn off the oven, and throw the sheet in. Leave it in there for 15 minutes to harden up and then serve. Store it in an airtight container or bag for up to a week, but it usually never lasts that long.

CHEAT SHEET:

Don't know how to pop corn on the stovetop? Heat 3 tablespoons of neutral oil in a large stockpot over medium heat. Add a couple kernels of the corn, put on the lid, and shake it around every now and then. Once one of them pops, that means your pan is ready. This might take up to a minute and a half. When the pan is hot, add ½ cup of corn kernels and cover that fucker up with a lid. If you have a glass lid, use that so you can supervise the corn. Shake the pan around every couple of seconds so things don't burn. It's like stirring without releasing all the heat. If the kernels don't start popping within the first 30 seconds, turn your heat up just a lil' bit. Soon, it should start to sound like motherfucking firecrackers. Once you hear more than a couple seconds between pops, turn off the heat. See? That took no fucking time at all.

Fresh Strawberry Coconut Balls

These are an updated take on the ubiquitous date and coconut balls you find in any old health-food store. We added strawberries to make them more interesting and to give the balls a soft pink hue. Because of the fresh fruit, you want to store them in the fridge, which also makes them the perfect dessert for the summer heat.

1 cup shredded coconut

¾ cup rolled oats

½ cup chopped fresh strawberries

¼ cup chopped almonds or cashews

4 soft dates, pits removed

¼ cup almond or cashew butter

1 Make the batter: Add the coconut, rolled oats, strawberries, chopped nuts, dates, and nut butter to a food processor and run that shit until everything looks smooth in there.

2 Line a baking sheet with parchment paper. Scoop out a Ping-Pong-ball-sized amount of batter and form a ball. Roll it around in a little shredded coconut and place it on the baking sheet. Keep going until you run out of batter. Place the balls in the fridge for at least an hour before serving. That's right—you don't have to bake shit. Rejoice. These are best eaten within 3 days of being made. Store any leftovers in an airtight container in the fridge.

FIELD GUIDE:
MELTING CHOCOLATE

There's plenty of occasions where you need to melt some chocolate. Lunch, dinner, during a work call, whenever. If you do that shit too quickly or use too high a heat, you'll end up with a bowl of grainy mud. Trust us, we learned the hard way. So follow our instructions, and dessert will be right around the fucking corner.

METHOD 1: MICROWAVE

You can melt chocolate quickly and use the fewest number of dishes by doing it this way. Chop up the chocolate, unless you are using chips, put them in a microwave-safe bowl, and heat in the microwave in 30-second increments, stirring after each until it's completely melted. The total length of time will depend on how much chocolate you're fucking with. Don't get crazy and try to do that shit in one big go because it'll get all messed up. We promise, we've been there. Just keep stirring it every 30 seconds and heating it again until it's all melted and you're good to go.

METHOD 2: DOUBLE BOILER

No microwave? No problem. You get to build your own double boiler like a motherfucking boss/grandma. Grab a medium saucepan and fill it with 2 to 3 inches of water. Throw an all-metal bowl on top of that and be sure the whole mouth of the pan is covered and that the water inside isn't touching the bottom of the metal bowl. Put this over medium-low heat and add the chopped chocolate or chips to the bowl. The steam will heat the bottom of the pan and melt the chocolate. Just keep stirring and trust the fucking method. When the chocolate looks all smooth, turn off the heat and take the bowl off the pan. Obviously, the bowl is gonna be hot as hell, so be careful.

Makes enough for 4 people / Cook time: 15 minutes, plus at least 1 hour chill time

Chocolate Peanut Butter Mousse

As vegans, we're used to getting the "where do you get your protein" question. Here it is. Mousse. We get our protein from rich, velvety mousse. Now please stop asking. We're giving you the recipe. What more do you want from us?

1 cup semisweet chocolate chips

¼ cup creamy peanut butter

2 teaspoons vanilla extract

2 blocks (12 ounces each) soft silken tofu*

½ cup plain or vanilla nondairy milk, whatever you've got

2 tablespoons agave or maple syrup

¼ teaspoon salt

Optional: chopped peanuts and chocolate shavings or extra chocolate chips

***You want the shelf-stable silken tofu, not the stuff packed in water in the cold case. You'll find it near the soy sauce at most grocery stores.**

1 Melt your chocolate (see Field Guide on page 191 for instructions), then stir in the peanut butter and vanilla until the peanut butter melts into the chocolate.

2 Grab your blender and throw in the tofu, milk, agave, salt, and the melted chocolate. Run that shit until it looks smooth, stopping to scrape down whatever melted chocolate gets stuck to the side. Done.

3 Pour this into a large bowl, cover, and set it in the fridge to cool and firm up. This needs at least 1 hour in the fridge to chill, but then it's ready to go.

4 Serve as is or topped with chopped peanuts and some chocolate shavings or chips. Or just grab a spoon and fuckin' enjoy. Here for a good time, not a long time, ya know?

Banana Fritters

We almost never fry desserts like this at home, but in the dark days of this world, there were very few places to find vegan donuts. Michelle had to find a way to feed her craving without a ton of work and without spending half her fucking day in the kitchen. These are the perfect, every-once-in-a-while treat to make when friends come over late for coffee or when you want to surprise your person with something decadent and special, made just for them.

2 ripe bananas

¾ cup nondairy milk

1 tablespoon ground flaxseeds

1½ cups all-purpose flour

2 tablespoons cane sugar

1¼ teaspoons baking powder

½ teaspoon salt

½ teaspoon ground cinnamon

¼ teaspoon ground nutmeg

¼ teaspoon ground ginger

Plain, unroasted peanut oil, for frying

Powdered sugar or maple syrup, for serving

1 Grab a medium bowl and mash the living fuck out of those bananas. Some chunks are fine, but keep them smaller than a nickel. Whisk them together with the milk and ground flaxseeds until they look well incorporated. In another medium bowl, whisk together the flour, cane sugar, baking powder, salt, cinnamon, nutmeg, and ginger. Now pour that flour mixture into the banana bowl and stir until everything is combined. The batter should be thick like you're making pancakes. (OK, you're on to us. Banana fritters are basically just fried banana pancakes. Doesn't that make you love them even more, though?)

2 Now for the sinful shit. Grab a medium pot or fryer with high sides and pour about 1 inch of oil in there. Warm it all up to medium-high heat. Do like grandma did and check if the oil is hot enough the old-fashioned way: Grab a wooden spoon and put the head of the spoon into the oil. If bubbles form around it, the oil is hot enough to fry. Sure, you could use a thermometer, but they take up so much fucking room in the utensil drawer and you rarely use it. This is the way to go.

(recipe continues)

3 Set a wire rack in a sheet pan lined with paper towels. Once the oil is hot enough, drop large dollops of batter the size of donut holes into the oil, 3 or 4 at a time depending on the size of your pot. Fry them until all their sides are golden brown, about a minute on each side. Place them on the rack over the paper towels.

4 Keep going until you run out of batter. You're gonna need to adjust the heat on the pan a little as you go. When you drop the cold batter into the oil, you bring down the heat of the pot, so you'll want to raise the heat *slightly* for the first minute of frying to get it to warm up and bring it down *slightly* toward the end of frying. Just pay attention. If you notice a batch of fritters taking way too fucking long in there to get golden, the oil got too cold. You'll figure it out.

5 When everything is all fried up, it's go time. These are best eaten ASAP. Serve warm, sprinkled with powdered sugar, or drizzle with maple syrup for a delicious mess.

WKND

Peach Custard Pie

Hold on just a goddamn minute. You saw a buncha words below and are probably thinking "nah, too complicated," but this is where the phrase "easy as pie" comes from (not exactly, but you catch our drift). If you're using a store-bought crust, hell, you're halfway done already. All that stands between you and this Southern dessert staple is a lil' bit of time.

½ recipe Flaky Pie Dough (recipe follows) or 1 store-bought unbaked pie crust

3 large peaches

3 tablespoons all-purpose flour

3 tablespoons brown sugar

Crumb Topping

1 cup rolled oats

¼ cup all-purpose flour

¼ cup almond or peanut butter

2 tablespoons olive oil

¼ cup cane sugar

¼ teaspoon ground cinnamon

¼ teaspoon salt

1 Warm your oven up to 400°F.

2 If you made your own dough, then you need to roll it out. Grab a 9-inch pie pan and roll out the dough on a well-floured surface until it's large enough to line the pie pan with 1 inch of dough hanging over the sides. Fold this over and pinch or crimp the edges of the crust down with the tines of a fork. Now it's time for the filling.

3 We are lazy and don't mind leaving the skin on the peaches. If you truly can't deal, peel them. Cut your peaches into half-moon slices, as thin as you can.

4 Sprinkle the flour and brown sugar into the pie shell. Layer your peaches into the pie shell in concentric circles, with the slices slightly leaning on top of one another. You just wanna get as many peach slices in there as you can and place them in some kind of reasonably neat arrangement. Figure it out.

5 Let's make the crumb topping: In your food processor, blitz together the rolled oats, flour, almond butter, olive oil, cane sugar, cinnamon, and salt until the oats are chopped up and the almond butter isn't sitting in a big clump.

(recipe and ingredients continue)

¼ **cup cane sugar**

2 tablespoons all-purpose flour

1 tablespoon cornstarch

½ **teaspoon ground cinnamon**

¼ **teaspoon ground nutmeg**

1 cup nondairy milk, warmed

1 tablespoon melted coconut oil or olive oil

1 teaspoon vanilla extract

No food processor? Just chop up the oats by hand and mix the rest of the ingredients in until everything looks incorporated. Easy shit.

6 Now make the custard filling: In a medium bowl or large glass, whisk together the cane sugar, flour, cornstarch, cinnamon, nutmeg, milk, coconut oil, and vanilla until there are no cornstarch clumps hiding out. Those fuckers can be sneaky, so look carefully. When the filling mixture is nice and smooth, pour it over the peach slices tucked in your prepared pie pan.

7 Crumble the topping over the pie, making sure to break up any almond butter clumps you might come across. Gently press the crumb topping into the pie filling just to make sure everything melds together.

8 Place the pie on a baking sheet and put that shit right in the oven. Bake your pie for 10 minutes at 400°F. Reduce the temperature to 350°F and bake until the edges of the crust look golden brown and the topping doesn't look wet in the center or jiggle easily when you tap the side of the pan, about 35 minutes.

9 Let the pie cool to at least room temperature before you dive in. You gotta let the custard firm up before you go to town. This is gonna depend on the temperature in your kitchen, so find a cool spot and leave it alone for at least 1 hour before checking on it. Serve cold or at room temp. Store leftovers in the fridge. They should last for at least 3 to 4 days.

CHEAT SHEET:

This pie is also delicious with canned peach halves if good fresh peaches aren't in season where you are. Just slice them into the recommended size. Plus, if you keep those fuckers in your pantry, you can have this pie ready in no time without even needing to go to the store.

Flaky Pie Dough

Makes 1 double crust /
Cook time: 1 hour 15 minutes, mostly inactive

2½ cups all-purpose flour

2 tablespoons cane sugar

½ teaspoon salt

1 stick (4 ounces) nondairy butter, chopped into chunks and frozen for at least 1 hour

4 tablespoons coconut oil or shortening, chopped into chunks and frozen for at least 1 hour

½ cup ice-cold water

If you're gonna go through the trouble of making a pie, that fucker should be DECADENT. This recipe makes one extra-flaky double crust, so if you only need a bottom crust, just halve the recipe. But if you wanna be clever you should just make it as is, wrap the extra dough in some plastic wrap and stick that shit in the freezer for a rainy day. Just let it thaw for a bit on the counter or in the fridge overnight before rolling it out.

1 In a medium bowl, stir together the flour, sugar, and salt.

2 Dump the chopped-up cold butter and coconut oil into the flour bowl. Using a pastry cutter or two big-ass forks, mush all the fat into the flour until there aren't any big chunks. It should look like clumpy sand with a bunch of pea-size pebbles of fat in it. If any of the fat starts melting too much, stick that entire fucking bowl back in the freezer for a few minutes so it can firm up. When you bake up the pie crust, those little fat pebbles are gonna melt, leaving little pockets in the crust and making it all flaky. That's why you wanna keep all this as cold as possible.

3 Sprinkle the flour with half of the ice water and stir until a shaggy ball of dough starts to come together. You want it to come together into a ball with as little water as possible because that can make it tough. Add as much of the rest of the water you need to make that shit happen. Pat it together into a ball and cut that shit into 2 roughly equal parts, then kinda pat them into sorta flat disks about as big around as a softball. Wrap each ball in plastic wrap or throw them in a resealable bag and keep them cold until you're ready to use them. You can keep the dough in the fridge for up to 3 days or the freezer for up to 3 months. To thaw the dough, let it sit in the fridge overnight.

Makes one 9-inch cake, enough for 1 to 10 people, depending on your lifestyle / Cook time: 1½ hours, mostly inactive

Fresh Pineapple Upside-Down Cake

This tropical-flavored treat will have people repeating, "Well, I usually don't like pineapple, but . . ." Don't give these haters a second slice.

Nondairy butter and flour, for the pan

4 tablespoons nondairy butter

½ cup packed brown sugar

2 tablespoons nondairy milk

3 rounds fresh pineapple,* less than ¼ inch thick

½ cup cane sugar

1 cup coconut milk

Grated zest of 2 limes

2 tablespoons fresh lime juice

1 teaspoon vanilla extract

½ teaspoon grated fresh ginger

2¼ cups all-purpose flour

1 teaspoon baking powder

1 teaspoon baking soda

½ teaspoon salt

½ teaspoon ground nutmeg

½ cup unsweetened shredded coconut

*We prefer fresh pineapple here, but canned would work. Grab the kind canned in juice, not syrup. That has no place in your pantry, k?

1 Warm the oven to 350°F. Grease and flour a 9-inch cake pan. Put a round of parchment paper on the bottom.

2 In a small saucepan, combine the 4 tablespoons nondairy butter and brown sugar and set over medium-low heat. Warm that up until the butter has melted and the sugar has dissolved, 3 to 4 minutes. When it looks caramelly, pour this into the prepared cake pan. Arrange the pineapple slices in the caramel in a single layer.

3 In a large bowl, whisk together the cane sugar and coconut milk until well combined and the sugar kinda starts to dissolve, about 1 minute. Add the lime zest, lime juice, vanilla, and ginger and whisk until everything is all mixed up. In a medium bowl, whisk together the flour, baking powder, baking soda, salt, and nutmeg.

4 Add the flour mixture to the bigger bowl in a couple batches so that you can mix it all in without a shit-ton of clumps. Fold in the shredded coconut.

5 Pour the batter over the pineapple slices as evenly as you can. Bake until the top looks golden and toothpick stuck in the center comes out clean, 40 to 50 minutes.

6 Now comes the hardest part: waiting. Let the cake cool in the pan for 30 minutes and then invert the cake onto a big plate so that the pineapple is on the top. Pull off the parchment. Let it cool completely, then serve.

Midnight Chocolate Cake with Milk Chocolate Ganache

Michelle dreamed this cake up one night while she was ransacking the kitchen with her wife, looking for something sweet. The cake is moist and almost velvety in texture. It's not too sweet, so the deep flavor the chocolate really shines. Basically, it's a classic chocolate cake that perfectly satisfies even the most mysterious of late-night munchies.

Chocolate Cake

Nondairy butter and flour, for the pans

1 cup nondairy milk

2 teaspoons apple cider vinegar or lemon juice

1¼ cups cane sugar

½ cup vanilla or plain nondairy yogurt

½ cup olive oil

1 teaspoon vanilla extract

1 cup hot coffee

2 cups all-purpose flour

¾ cup unsweetened cocoa powder*

1½ teaspoons baking powder

1 teaspoon baking soda

½ teaspoon salt

1 Make the cake: Warm your oven up to 350°F. Grease and flour two 8-inch round cake pans. Set that shit aside.

2 In a small glass, stir together the milk and vinegar. Grab a large bowl and whisk together the sugar, yogurt, olive oil, and vanilla until they look sorta combined. Add the milk mixture to the sugar mixture and whisk again until everything is all combined. Pour in the hot coffee and whisk all the liquids together one last time. In a medium bowl, whisk together the flour, cocoa powder, baking powder, baking soda, and salt. Fold the dry ingredients into the wet ingredients until they're just combined.

3 Divide the batter evenly between the two cake pans. Bake until a toothpick stuck into the middle of each layer comes out clean, 30 to 35 minutes. Let the cakes cool in the pans for 10 minutes then remove them and place them on a wire rack to continue cooling. Let both cake layers cool completely before frosting.

(recipe and ingredients continue)

Milk Chocolate Ganache

1½ cups canned coconut cream

1½ cups semisweet chocolate chips or chopped semisweet chocolate

For Topping (optional)

Fresh strawberries or raspberries

*You want regular cocoa powder, not Dutch process cocoa. That's a whole other beast.

4 Make the ganache: Warm up the canned coconut cream on the stove or in the microwave until it's hot. Place the chocolate in a metal bowl and pour the hot cream over it. Let it sit, without stirring, for 2 minutes so that the cream can low-key melt the chocolate. Now whisk them together until all the chocolate is melted and the ganache starts to thicken up. Let that cool for 1 hour or so until it's thick enough to smear with a spoon. (Chocolate not melting for some reason? Make a double boiler—see page 191—to help it along.)

5 To frost the cake, place one of the cooled cake layers on a plate, top side up. Pour or spoon over some of the cooled ganache, then place the other cake layer on top, top side up. Putting the two domed tops of the cake together means your cake is more likely to turn out lopsided or uneven because it won't be stable. Learn from our mistakes. Spoon more ganache over the top and along the sides of the cake with a butter knife or offset spatula. If you want, top with fresh strawberries or raspberries. Now chill that shit or leave it in a cool spot to help the ganache set. Serve or give it a night in the fridge to get extra fudgy. It's fucking delicious either way.

CHEAT SHEET:

Wanna be extra fancy? Melt some chocolate (see Melting Chocolate, page 191) and pour it down the sides as you see fit. It not only looks decadent but also covers up any frosting fuck-ups you might have. A rare win-win.

Co-op Carrot Cake with Vanilla Frosting

This is dirty hippie baking at its finest: carrot cake with tofu frosting. Before you roll your eyes, just know that this satisfies all your sweet cravings without making you crash in an hour from the ass-load of sugar you just inhaled. Plus, you'll be getting some protein. This is basically health food.

Carrot Cake

Nondairy butter and flour, for the pans

2½ cups grated carrots

1 can (15 ounces) coconut milk

1 cup orange juice

2 tablespoons olive oil

1 tablespoon vanilla extract

3 cups all-purpose flour

1 cup cane sugar

2 teaspoons baking powder

1 teaspoon baking soda

2 teaspoons ground cinnamon

1 teaspoon ground ginger

½ teaspoon ground nutmeg

½ teaspoon salt

1 cup chopped dried fruit, such as golden raisins or pineapple

½ cup chopped nuts, such as pecans or macadamia nuts

1 Make the cake: Warm up your oven to 375°F. Grease and flour two 8-inch round cake pans.

2 In a medium bowl, mix together the carrots, coconut milk, orange juice, olive oil, and vanilla. In a large bowl, whisk together the flour, cane sugar, baking powder, baking soda, cinnamon, ginger, nutmeg, and salt. Nothing too hard. Now pour the carrot mixture into the flour mixture and stir them together until they are just combined and there aren't any big dry spots. Sprinkle on the dried fruit and nuts, then fold them into the batter.

3 Divide the batter evenly between the prepared cake pans and throw them in the oven. Bake the cake layers until a toothpick stuck into the center of each cake pan comes out clean, 30 to 40 minutes. Let the cake layers cool for 10 minutes in their pans.

4 After 10 minutes, turn the cake layers out onto a wire rack to continue cooling. Be sure the layers have cooled completely before frosting them. Otherwise, the shit will just melt everywhere or the hot cake will absorb it all.

Creamy Vanilla Frosting

6 ounces extra-firm silken tofu*

½ cup powdered sugar

2 tablespoons coconut oil

2 teaspoons fresh lemon juice

2 teaspoons vanilla extract

Pinch of salt

***You want the shelf-stable silken tofu, not the stuff packed in water in the cold case. You'll find it near the soy sauce at most grocery stores.**

5 Make the frosting: Grab a food processor or blender and toss in the tofu, powdered sugar, coconut oil, lemon juice, vanilla, and salt. Let that shit run until it looks all smooth, up to 1 minute. The frosting will look like a thick pudding, so don't freak the fuck out. That's exactly what you want. Remember, this is some old-school hippie shit.

6 Place one cooled cake on the center of a large plate and smear a bunch of the frosting all over the top, then put the other cake layer on top of it and add more frosting. Leave the sides naked in all their glory. Serve it right away or stick it back in the fridge to chill.

Lemon Almond Blondies with Basil Sugar

This recipe started out as a Bundt cake, but it just wasn't hitting the spot that we wanted it to. After several attempts with odd results, we arrived at this summer blondie. The herbaceous basil takes these bars to the next level and makes them an unforgettable addition to any table full of bullshit boxed desserts at the next potluck you're forced to attend.

Nondairy butter and flour, for the baking pan

4 tablespoons nondairy butter or coconut oil, melted

¼ cup vanilla or plain nondairy yogurt

¾ cup packed brown sugar

2 tablespoons nondairy milk

2 tablespoon ground flaxseeds

Grated zest of 1 lemon

1 teaspoon vanilla extract

1 teaspoon almond extract

1 cup all-purpose flour

½ teaspoon baking powder

¼ teaspoon baking soda

¼ teaspoon ground cinnamon

¼ teaspoon salt

¼ cup coarsely chopped almonds

2 tablespoons Basil Sugar (recipe follows), plus more for sprinkling

1 Warm up your oven to 350°F. Grease and flour an 8-inch square baking pan. For extra insurance, line the pan with parchment paper, leaving flaps hanging over two opposite sides of the pan to use as your lifting belt. Set the pan aside.

2 In a medium bowl, whisk together the melted butter, yogurt, and brown sugar. Now whisk in the milk, flaxseeds, lemon zest, vanilla, and almond extract until everything looks evenly distributed. In a small bowl, whisk together the flour, baking powder, baking soda, cinnamon, and salt. Dump the flour mixture into the yogurt mixture and mix it all up until it's just combined and there aren't any big clumps of flour. Sprinkle on the almonds and stir just until they are evenly distributed.

3 Spread the batter evenly into the prepared pan. The batter will be thick. Make small cuts on the top of the batter with a butter knife and sprinkle the basil sugar into the cuts, pressing the sugar down into the batter. Bake until a toothpick stuck into the center of the blondies comes out clean and the edges look golden brown, 20 to 25 minutes.

4 Let them cool in the pan for 15 minutes before removing. Sprinkle with more basil sugar and serve warm or at room temperature.

Basil Sugar

Makes ½ cup / Cook time: 5 minutes

½ cup cane sugar

¼ cup packed fresh basil leaves

This is great sprinkled over fresh tomatoes, on top of our Morning Cornbread (page 28), or on the rims of glasses of lemonade or your favorite summer cocktails.

Throw the basil and sugar in a food processor and pulse until the basil has disappeared into the sugar and everything looks bright green. Store in an airtight container and use within 1 week.

Hazelnut Butter Cake

There's something about a dessert with hazelnuts that screams "I'm a fancy adult with refined taste and my shit's together." That might not be true, but this cake is well worth the minimal effort it takes to throw it together. Let your friends and family think you live a life of ease and luxury. Fake it 'til you bake it, right?

Nondairy butter and flour, for the pan

1 cup nondairy milk

1 teaspoon apple cider vinegar

1 cup all-purpose flour

½ cup hazelnut flour,* plus more for dusting

2 tablespoons cornstarch

1 teaspoon baking powder

½ teaspoon baking soda

¼ teaspoon salt

2 tablespoons melted nondairy butter, coconut oil, or olive oil

2 tablespoons olive oil

¼ cup cane sugar

¼ cup packed brown sugar

1 tablespoon hazelnut liqueur or nondairy milk

1 teaspoon vanilla extract

1 teaspoon almond extract

Powdered sugar, for dusting

*You don't need a fancy market to find this. Just process ¾ cup hazelnuts, skinned or not, in a food processor until it creates a fine flour. Run the flour through a fine-mesh sieve to take out any big chunks.

1 Warm up your oven to 350°F. Grease and flour an 8-inch cake pan.

2 In a small glass, whisk together the nondairy milk and vinegar. In a medium bowl, whisk together the all-purpose flour, hazelnut flour, cornstarch, baking powder, baking soda, and salt. In a large bowl, whisk together the melted butter, olive oil, cane sugar, and brown sugar until they're well incorporated. Add the hazelnut liqueur, vanilla, and almond extract. Stir in the milk mixture. And finally, stir in the flour mixture until there are no more big flour chunks. There, that was the hardest part.

3 Pour the batter into the prepared cake pan. Bake until a toothpick stuck into the middle comes out clean, 30 to 35 minutes. Let the cake cool in the pan for 10 minutes and then remove it and place it on a wire rack to finish. Let the cake cool completely before serving.

4 To serve, top the cake with a dusting of powdered sugar and hazelnut flour.

CHEAT SHEET:

Want to take it to the next level? Drizzle over our Milk Chocolate Ganache (from Midnight Chocolate Cake, page 201), then sprinkle hazelnut flour around the rim of the cake. It looks fancy, but it's easy as fuck.

Chocolate Raspberry Babka

Fair warning: This shit is probably our most time-consuming recipe, but what else are you gonna do? Scroll thru the Internet with that joyless expression on your face? Nah, that's not productive or delicious. So let's make a motherfuckin' babka. You'll have something to put on your feed. Plus ya know, you get a babka.

Dough

1 envelope (2¼ teaspoons) active dry yeast

¾ cup nondairy milk, warmed but not hot

½ cup plus a pinch of cane sugar

4½ cups all-purpose flour

½ teaspoon salt

½ cup vanilla or plain nondairy yogurt (other flavors work— just don't go wild)

1 stick (4 ounces) nondairy butter, at room temperature

Safflower or other neutral oil, for greasing the bowl

Nondairy butter and flour, for the baking pan

Filling

1 cup semisweet or dark chocolate chips

4 tablespoons nondairy butter

1½ cups frozen or fresh raspberries, no need to thaw if frozen

2 tablespoons cane sugar

1 You gotta start with the dough: Yeah, this is a long recipe, but chill out. It's fucking worth it otherwise we wouldn't have put this shit in here. OK, ready? In a glass, stir the yeast into the warmed milk with a pinch of sugar and set it aside. If you see it looking a little foamy at the top of the glass, it means your yeast is alive and you're good to go. Don't see that foam? Stop and go buy some new yeast.

2 In a stand mixer with the dough hook, stir together 4 cups of the flour, the remaining ½ cup sugar, and the salt until they're all mixed up. (You could do this all by hand if you don't have a stand mixer. It's just gonna be a workout when you need to knead this shit.) Make a well in the center of the flour and add the yeast mixture and yogurt. Start mixing until something that kinda looks like a dough starts to come together. Then with the mixer on low (or mixing slowly with a large spoon), add the butter, a soft spoonful at a time, mixing until all the butter has disappeared into the dough, scraping down the sides of the bowl as needed. Beat on high for 10 minutes, until the dough looks smooth and has a little stretch to it when you try to tear a small piece off. (If you're doing this by hand, turn the dough out onto a well-floured surface and knead the hell out of it for 15 to 20 minutes to achieve the same results.) If the dough is

(recipe and ingredients continue)

3 tablespoons maple syrup

2 tablespoons nondairy butter, melted

Note: You could replace the raspberries with any berries you think will taste good with chocolate, like blackberries or blueberries. It's gonna be gorgeous either way.

too sticky and isn't forming a smooth ball, add some of the remaining ½ cup flour, while it's being kneaded, a couple tablespoons at a time until it shapes up. Too dry looking? Do the same shit with some milk or water.

3 When the dough is looking good, place it in an oiled bowl, turning once to coat the top with oil so it doesn't dry out. Cover and let it rise in a warm place until it roughly doubles in size, 1 to 1½ hours.

4 When the dough is almost ready to go, make the filling: Melt the chocolate chips in a double boiler or the microwave (see Melting Chocolate, page 191). Add the butter to the melted chocolate and stir until everything is melted and mixed together. Remove from the heat.

5 In a food processor or by hand, pulse or roughly chop the raspberries with the sugar.

6 Butter and flour one 9 × 13-inch baking pan. Line the bottom with some parchment paper as extra insurance.

7 OK, this is the hardest part, but you've got this shit. Punch down the dough, knead it once or twice, and place it on a well-floured surface. Roll the dough out to a 10 × 16-inch rectangle, keeping a long side facing you. Now, spread the cooled chocolate mixture evenly over the dough but leave a ½-inch border around the edges (so it will look nicer when you roll it up). Sprinkle the chopped-up berries as evenly as you can over the chocolate layer. Now we roll. Dip your fingertips in water and wet the border of dough on the far side of the rectangle. Starting at the long side near you, roll the dough up with the filling into a long, tight burrito shape with the ends open. Press that edge you got wet into the dough a little bit so it kinda seals shut (A). Is your chocolate already running all over the place and you're a fucking mess? Stick that log in the freezer for 10 to 15 minutes to cool off and go clean your ass up.

8 Now we shape. Place the log of dough down in front of you with a short side facing you. Gently slice the log in half lengthwise, leaving the very top (the short side away from

(recipe continues)

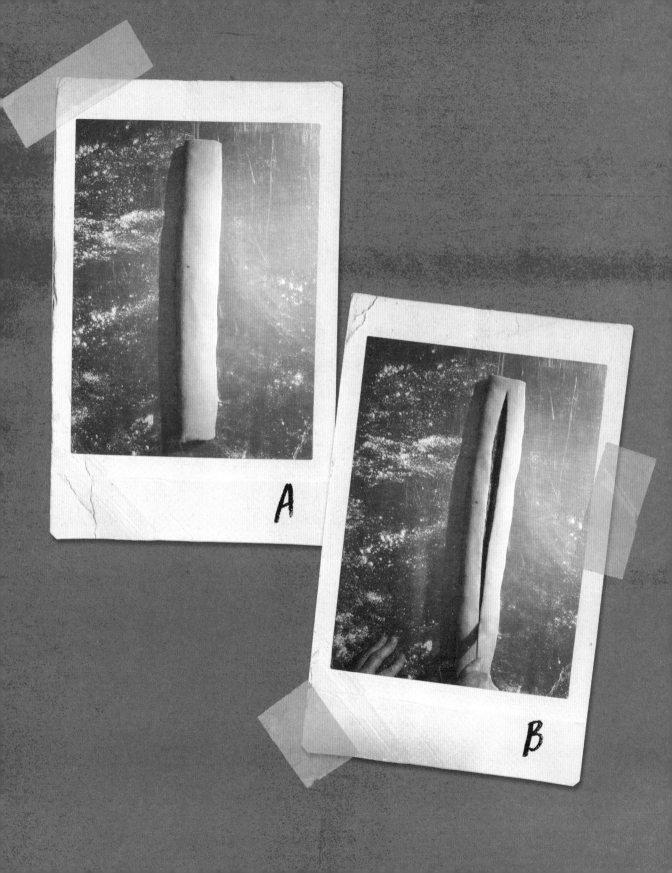

C

D

you) still connected by about ½ inch of dough (B). Now we do a lazy braid. Lift one side over the next, forming a twist and trying to keep the cut sides facing out, so you can see the layers, not hiding underneath (C). WHAT WOULD BE THE FUCKING POINT OF ALL THIS THEN? SHOW OFF, DAMMIT. Pinch and tuck the end of the braid down under the loaf, do the same to the noncut edge too (D), and place the whole loaf gently in the prepared baking pan. It's okay if the braid isn't crazy tight, because we've got to let this rise one more time and it will puff up and fill some of those gaps.

9 Cover the loaf and place the baking pan with the dough back in that warm place and let it rise for 30 minutes to 1 hour, or until it has almost doubled in size and looks nice and fluffy and basically like a big-ass loaf of bread. When it's almost ready, warm up the oven to 375°F.

10 Bake the braid until a toothpick stuck in without resistance comes out clean, 30 to 40 minutes.

11 While the babka is baking, make the glaze: In a small glass, mix together the maple syrup and melted better.

12 When you pull the loaf from the oven, gently brush the whole loaf with the maple glaze and let it cool for 15 minutes in the pan. Pull it out of the pan and let it cool down the rest of the way on a wire rack.

13 This babka is prettiest the day it's baked, but it will keep for 4 or 5 days in the fridge. It also freezes fucking perfectly, so double the recipe and stash a baked one away for later. Eat it within 3 months. Thaw it in the fridge overnight, then let it come to room temperature on the counter before digging in.

Maple Pull-Apart Monkey Bread

Think of this as a cake made of donut holes. Yes, we know it's called monkey bread, but that's just because you pull it apart with your fingers like a chimpanzee. Focus on the delicious dessert coming your way, not the weird name.

Dough

1 envelope (2¼ teaspoons) instant yeast

1½ cups nondairy milk like almond, warm but not hot

½ teaspoon salt

2 tablespoons cane sugar

½ cup melted nondairy butter or coconut oil, plus more for greasing the bowl

4 cups all-purpose flour

2 tablespoons ground flaxseeds

½ teaspoon ground cinnamon

¼ teaspoon ground nutmeg

Assembly

½ cup cane sugar

2 tablespoons cinnamon

½ cup melted nondairy butter or coconut oil, plus more for greasing the pan

All-purpose flour, for the pan

½ cup maple syrup

1 In a medium glass, mix the yeast and the warm milk together. If the yeast starts looking a little foamy after a few minutes, then you're good to keep going. If nothing looks different, then the milk was too hot and your yeast got straight up COOKED. Start over. You can't cook in a crime scene. Once the yeast is looking right, whisk in the salt, sugar, and ½ cup melted butter. In the bowl of your stand mixer, whisk together the flour, flaxseeds, cinnamon, and nutmeg.

2 With your dough hook attached to the stand mixer, run it on low as you slowly add the butter and milk mixture to the bowl. Once all the flour is mixed in, turn the speed up to medium and let the machine knead the dough until it looks like a smooth ball, 7 to 10 minutes. You can also do this by hand, but you're just gonna have to work a little harder and knead the dough for double the time, okay? Totally your call. Grease a large bowl and place the dough inside, cover it with a clean dishtowel, then let it sit in a warm spot until it doubles in size, about 1 hour.

3 While the dough is rising, stir the cane sugar and cinnamon together in a small bowl. Heat up the oven to 350°F, then grease and flour your favorite Bundt pan. When the dough is ready to go, punch it down and knead it a few times to get it back into a ball shape. Pull off a piece about the size of a Ping-Pong ball and form a ball. Roll this ball in the cinnamon and sugar mixture then place it in the prepared Bundt pan. Keep going until you fill the pan and run out of dough.

4 Whisk together the maple syrup and remaining ½ cup melted butter, then pour this over the dough in the Bundt pan. Stick this in the oven and bake it until the top looks golden brown, 30 to 40 minutes. Let the pull-apart bread cool in the pan for 10 minutes, then cover the open top of the pan with a large plate and invert the pan to free the bread from the pan. Serve warm or at room temperature. Store leftovers in the fridge. This will keep for about 3 days before it starts to lose it deliciousness.

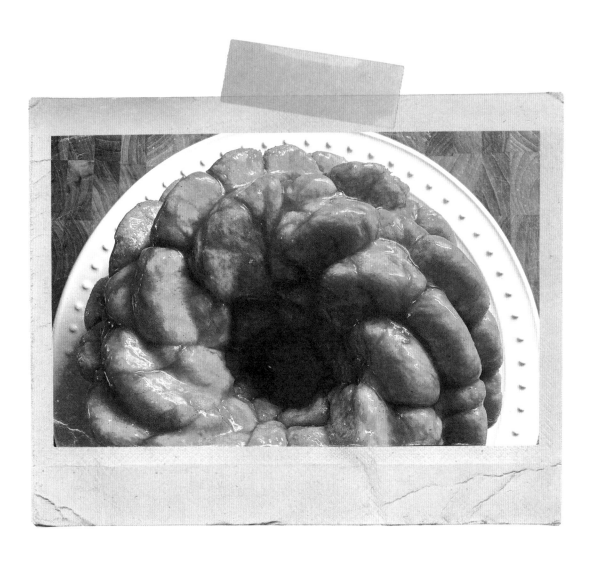

Culinary Side-Quests

Back here is where we've stashed some extra kitchen info that we think you should know as budding home chefs. These pages are full of all kinds of tips and tricks that will help you freestyle a meal or cook something out of your imagination with success. Bookmark this section for quick reference because this information will help you, no matter what's for dinner.

Basically, if you had a follow-up question to any of our recipes in this book, we've probably explained that shit back here. Read through it and feel your culinary powers grow stronger by the minute.

GRAINS

Cooking grains tends to go quicker than cooking beans (see Sunday Beans, page 155), but these motherfuckers require a little more maintenance. Just like beans, know that they're gonna increase in volume when you cook 'em, so 1 cup uncooked rice will give you 3 cups cooked. Use the following guides to get some grains going, just be sure to adjust that shit for how much you need for whatever you're making. If you ever end up with extra water in the pot when your grains are done, just drain that shit off. You don't wanna cook until the grains are all mushy but the water is gone. That foolishness ends here. Also, if you run out of water and your grains aren't done, just pour more in. You're not gonna fuck anything up. You got this. WE BELIEVE IN YOU AND WE'VE NEVER EVEN MET.

Barley

This grain is nutty, chewy, and highly underrated. Not only is it full of fiber, but it's packed with selenium, copper, and manganese, so you know you're getting your money's worth. There are two main kinds of barley you're gonna run into at the store: hulled and pearled. Hulled takes longer to cook but has more fiber and other good shit than the pearled variety, which has that stuff polished off. Pearled barley is super creamy and easier to find in most stores, so just use what you've got. For hulled barley, combine 1 cup of the grain with 3 cups water in a saucepan with a pinch of salt. Bring to a boil, then cover and simmer that shit until it's tender, 40 to 50 minutes. For pearled, keep the grain-to-water ratio the same, but simmer it uncovered until it's tender, about 25 minutes. Want it less creamy? Just rinse that shit when it's done cooking.

Couscous

This cooks quickly since technically it's a pasta, not a grain. Don't believe us? Look that shit up. These mini motherfuckers will be ready in 10 minutes flat. Throw 1 cup couscous into a pot or bowl with a lid and a pinch of salt. Add 1¼ cups boiling water, stir, and throw that lid on. No heat under the pot or nothing. Just let that sit for 8 minutes, then fluff the couscous with a fork and serve. Fucking done.

Farro

Farro is a type of old-timey wheat that is similar in texture to barley but with larger, longer grains. Farro is nearly always sold pearled in North America, which means the bran has been removed. This means it needs less cooking time than regular or semi-pearled farro, which retains some of the bran and is the most common variety found in Italy. You can also soak whole farro overnight to shorten the cooking time if you're into that sort of thing. You can find it in the bulk section or near the rice in a well-stocked grocery store. Bring 1 cup of farro to boil with 3 cups of salted water. If it's pearled, it should taste chewy but soft after 15 to 20 minutes. If you get regular farro, you'll need 30 to 40 minutes. Drain off any extra water and serve warm, stir it into a soup, or chill for a filling salad add-in.

Millet

Yeah, this kinda looks like birdseed (because it technically is), but it's cheap as fuck and deserves more love in the kitchen. It's like a cross between quinoa and brown rice and worthy of a test run on your plate. Throw 1 cup of millet in a medium pot over medium heat and sauté it around until it smells toasty, about 2 minutes. Add 2 cups water and a pinch of salt and simmer that shit, covered, until the millet is tender, 25 to 35 minutes.

Quinoa

Some people cook this protein-packed grain like rice, but you should treat it like pasta. To cook, rinse the quinoa in a sieve, then bring 2 cups water to boil in a medium pot with a pinch of salt, drop in ½ cup quinoa and simmer, uncovered, until the quinoa is tender, 15 to 20 minutes. Drain off any water that's left.

Brown Rice

You might think this is some hippie health food, but it packs way more health benefits and flavor than white rice. We've always got a big pot of cooked brown rice in the fridge, and your ass should, too. Shit, you could even freeze it into whatever portions you like and heat it up as you need it. If you're still giving this motherfucker the side-eye, try out the short-grain variety (see the recipe at right). That nutty, delicious son of a bitch will make you forget white rice altogether. You can cook the long-grain variety in the same way, but that shit is gonna take about 15 minutes longer and an extra ½ cup water.

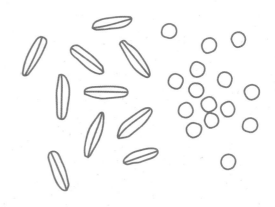

Basic Pot of Brown Rice

Make about 4 cups /
Cook time: 40 minutes

1 teaspoon olive or coconut oil (optional)*
2 cups short-grain brown rice
Pinch of salt
3½ cups water

*This oil business is optional, but it gives the rice a nuttier taste. Your call, champ.

1 In a medium saucepan, heat the oil (if using) over medium heat. Add the rice and sauté that shit until it smells a little nutty, about 2 minutes. Add the salt and water and stir. Bring to a simmer, then reduce the heat, cover, and let this very softly simmer until all the water is absorbed and the rice is tender, about 35 minutes.

2 Did you fuck up the heat and the rice is tender but there's still water? Just drain that shit. Is the rice not done but all the water is gone? Just stir in more a little more water, turn the heat down, and keep going. Don't let some tiny-ass rice get you off your game. YOU. GOT. THIS.

WTF INGREDIENTS

Every now and then a recipe will call for an ingredient that will stop you dead in your tracks. Instead of throwing up your hands and giving up, we encourage you to learn some shit about this new foodstuff so you can add it to your repertoire. It's not that hard. Here's a list of the most uncommon stuff we call for, why, and where to find it.

BRAGG LIQUID AMINOS: Yeah, more hippie shit. It tastes and looks a lot like soy sauce but has a little something extra that's hard to explain. It's fucking delicious though, and something you should keep on hand. Plus, it's gluten-free. You can find this sauce near the soy sauce or vinegars at most stores or, again, on the goddamn Internet.

CHIPOTLE PEPPERS IN ADOBO SAUCE: These smoked jalapeño peppers packed in sauce add a slow-cooked taste to even the fastest of meals. You'll almost never use the whole can at once, so freeze the rest of that shit and thaw when you need them. When you chop the chipotles, cut them open and scrape out the seeds. If you prefer it hot, then keep some of the seeds in, but think of your butthole tomorrow when you make that call. They are sold in tiny cans, usually near the salsa and beans at the store. Buy an extra to always keep on hand. Trust us.

CRYSTALIZED CITRIC ACID: We love adding a citric tang to food in three main ways: with lemon juice, with lime juice, and with straight-up citric acid crystals, aka sour salt. Usually used in food as a preservative, citric acid sprinkled in a pot of rice before or after it's cooked adds a certain something that people can't quite put their finger on. Adding acid to dishes is one of the biggest differences between home-cooked meals and restaurant dishes. Restaurants always do this, and you should too. Fresh lemon and lime juice are great and super easy to drizzle over dishes that are tasting flat. Vinegars are fabulous, too. But our real favorite is citric acid crystals. You can buy this in bulk online or in the vitamin section of some stores, and it's very affordable. Seriously, it's cheap as shit, and since you only use a little at a time, it'll last you awhile. Toss it along with some salt onto potatoes before you roast them. Add it to your favorite sauces and use it with some salt to rim your margaritas. We use it on almost everything, and we fucking swear, you will, too. But a little pinch goes a long way, so don't overdo it and end up ruining a meal. Start with ¼ teaspoon, taste, then add more as needed.

LIQUID SMOKE: This shit does exactly what you think it does: adds a smoky flavor to whateverthefuck you're cooking up. It is made by collecting the smoke from burning wood chips, letting that cool, and adding a little water to the mix. It adds a shit-ton of flavor but is easy to overdo, so go slow when you're measuring that shit out. Sure, you can do this yourself if you are crazy about that DIY shit, but just buy a bottle and save yourself the work. It's in a bottle near the BBQ sauce at the store, so stop thinking you can't find it. It's there.

MISO: Miso paste is made of fermented soybeans, or other beans, and grains and comes in a bunch of fucking flavors, depending on what is added during the fermentation process and how long it's all fermented for. For example, red miso usually has barley added to the rice and soybeans in most misos, while a mellow white miso usually is fermented for a shorter time than other misos. Because it's fermented, miso is full of probiotics and all that good shit that's great for your gut, so add it last to soup or anything hot so you don't overheat it and kill all that good stuff. Always salty but sometimes sweet, miso is a great way to add depth to the flavor of a meal that will make your guests think you're a fucking magician in the kitchen. You can find it in the fridge at a well-stocked store. The packaging will tell you whether it's a sweeter miso or something with a deeper flavor, so buy what you will use. Anything stored on a shelf ain't worth your time or your money.

NOOCH: Nutritional yeast, or nooch if you're cool like that, is some real throwback hippie shit. It's deactivated yeast sold in flakes that makes everything taste kinda cheesy. It's packed with vitamin B$_{12}$, folate, selenium, zinc, and protein. You can find it in bulk bins at some grocery stores, near the soy sauce in jars sometimes, and on the Internet. It is not the same thing as brewer's yeast, which you don't ever fucking need.

PANKO BREAD CRUMBS: There are regular bread crumbs and then there's panko, their much more glamorous older sister. Panko crumbs are much lighter than traditional bread crumbs and are broken into large, coarse flakes rather than tiny-ass-sand-looking pieces. The crumbs are used to coat all types of fried and baked shit because they stay crisper longer than most bread crumbs. You can grab a box of these fuckers somewhere near the soy sauce in your grocery store or near the rest of the bread crumbs.

TOFU: Everybody knows what this is, but most people have no fucking clue how it's made or how to fucking cook it. Tofu is made from soy milk that has been curdled and then drained of the liquid. The remaining solid stuff is molded into bricks. Served alone, it can be soft and have no fucking flavor, so think of it more as something that needs to be fucking seasoned rather than as an ingredient that's bringing any flavor to the table. One cup of tofu has 20 grams of protein, is rich in calcium and iron, and is cholesterol-free, so stop being afraid and try this fucker out at home. You can find it in the fridge packed in water and in aseptic containers near the soy sauce at the store.

TAHINI: This creamy deliciousness is just like peanut butter except made out of sesame seeds. Think you've never had it? If you've had hummus, then you're fucking wrong. Tahini is a crucial ingredient in any hummus worth eating, but you'll find it used in plenty of other tasty-as-hell ways all over the world. Grab it near the falafel mix or by the peanut butter at the store and keep it on hand from now on.

UME PLUM VINEGAR: This is absolutely the hardest thing to find on this list but if you see this shit, BUY IT. BUY LOTS OF IT. It's not expensive and a little goes a long way, but even in Los Angeles, we've had to give up and buy it online. This vinegar is the salty brine left over from making umeboshi, aka pickled Japanese green plums. It's addictive. It tastes more like a salty liquid than any type of vinegar you've ever had. It brings a buttload (technical term) of umami to the table, disappears into whatever you add it, and elevates every flavor. It will make people wonder why the fuck your food always tastes better than theirs. Sprinkle a little over roasted veggies as they come out of the oven, add it to soup, throw some over salad, mix it in with tomato sauce or mac and cheese—literally everywhere. A light sprinkle of ume plum vinegar on your saddest, laziest dinner will suddenly make it fucking delicious. We had almost never put it in our recipes until this book because it can be hard to find, but trust us, it ends up in so much of our food. This is the ultimate secret ingredient.

PANTRY PRIMER

Cooking from what you have on hand is a great goal as a new home chef. But first, you've got to stock your kitchen. Here we piled together a list of simple shit you need to be able to cook a basic meal like the true effortless god that you are. We know it looks kinda long, but trust us, you'll use all of it if you're cooking like you should. These are items we always keep stocked so that there's always something we can make for dinner. This is basic grocery store shit, so you shouldn't have to change up your shopping routine to find most of this stuff. When in doubt, order it online. Now make a list, get your ass to the store, and be nice as fuck to the cashier. They could probably use it. Unless you've bagged groceries to pay bills, you don't how insane customers are. Don't be one of the weird ones, k?

Basic Dried Herbs and Spices
- All-purpose, no-salt seasoning blend
- Basil
- Black pepper
- Chili powder
- Cinnamon
- Coriander
- Cumin
- Garlic granules or garlic powder
- Onion powder
- Oregano
- Red pepper flakes
- Salt
- Smoked paprika
- Turmeric
- Thyme
- Yellow curry powder (no-salt)

Pantry Shit
- Olive oil (we use extra-virgin olive oil everywhere it says olive oil in here because we love that shit)
- A neutral-tasting oil: plain peanut or avocado
- Soy sauce or tamari
- Braggs Liquid Aminos
- A nut/seed butter you prefer: peanut, almond, tahini, whatever
- Rice vinegar
- One other basic vinegar you prefer: apple cider, balsamic, white wine, whateverthefuck you find
- Ume plum vinegar (see page 222)
- Your favorite grain: short-grain brown rice and jasmine are both favorites around here
- Your favorite pasta noodles
- Canned low-sodium diced tomatoes
- Tomato passata or strained tomatoes
- Your favorite dried and canned beans (keep both stocked for when you can take your time and when you're in a hurry)
- Your go-to flour: all-purpose, whole wheat pastry, rice, whatever your favorite shit is
- Cane sugar
- Maple syrup or agave
- A favorite vegetable broth or stock base

Vegetable Basics

- Yellow onions
- Garlic bulbs
- Carrots
- Some kind of leafy green, such as cabbage, spinach, romaine, or kale
- Fresh herbs: chives, cilantro, green onions, dill, or whatever you like
- Frozen green peas or edamame
- Frozen broccoli
- Fresh citrus like lemons and/or limes

If you're able to keep most of this at your place, you should always be able to make something to eat even if the fridge looks bare. Don't stress if you can't get this all at once because money is tight. It takes time to get your pantry set up, so be patient with yourself and keep a running list of what you need on your phone. That will: (1) keep you from overbuying shit you already have, and (2) help you make sure you're grabbing exactly what you need when shit goes on sale. Lock in your basics now and you'll be able to cook and shop without a list in no time.

FAT 411

When it comes to cooking and baking, not all oils are created equal or work for every job. We use extra-virgin olive oil for 90 percent of cooking and baking in our kitchen, but occasionally we reach for something else. Y'all should understand why, so here's a quick rundown on what to use and where to use it. No matter what you pick, heat your oils up until they shimmer, then you can get to cooking. Smoking means your shit is too hot, so turn it down or use another oil because you already fucked it up. Got a really nice extra-virgin olive oil? Save it for drizzling on salads or adding to cooked items right at the end so that great fresh flavor doesn't get lost by being heated.

Avoid

Right out the gate, DO NOT go buying some bullshit like these:

- Vegetable oil
- Any partially hydrogenated oils
- Canola oil

Most of these oils are highly refined and offer no nutritional trade-off. Grab something else and get your money's worth.

Low- to Medium-Heat Oils

- Extra-virgin olive oil
- Unrefined/virgin coconut oil (this one tastes like coconut; stable at room temp)
- Any of the high-heat oils (see below)

High-Heat Oils

- Refined coconut oil (no coconut taste; stable at room temp)
- Plain peanut oil
- Avocado oil

Oils for Drizzling, Dressings, and Extra Flavor

- Extra-virgin olive oil
- Toasted sesame oil
- Avocado oil
- Nondairy butter sticks

Everyday Veggie Cheat Sheet

Sometimes you just need an extra veggie on the table, but you don't wanna go searching for a new, elaborate recipe. We get it. Here's a list of some common vegetables and our favorite ways to cook them without much effort. Where we think you need to know about a specific recipe, we've pointed you in that direction. But here's to keeping shit simple, whenever and wherever we can. Just remember when cooking veggies, you wanna be sure to use a big pan so the veggies have room to breathe. If you pile everything in a sauté pan or sheet pan that's too small, they not only cook unevenly but basically just steam. Pick a larger cooking container and everything will get cooked to perfection because it will have a direct relationship to heat. It's pretty simple.

Broccoli

Broccoli is an all-star side dish if you cook it right. Follow our instructions and let your love for it grow.

SAUTÉING: We love sautéing it in a little olive oil with some all-purpose seasoning, until it's fork-tender, then sprinkling it with some salt and lemon juice.

ROASTING: Roasting broccoli allows it to take on a nuttier dimension. Sub broccoli in for the cauliflower in Sheet Pan Cauliflower with Pumpkin Seeds (page 102) for a surprising treat and a solid and easy roasting recipe, or you can stick your broccoli in the oven tossed with a little oil at 400°F for about 25 minutes.

STEAMING: Lightly steam it, then stick it on the skewers with the Torn Tofu Satay (page 159) for some extra-special kebabs. Or fuck it, steam it on the stove until fork-tender, about 12 minutes, then eat it with the sunflower butter sauce from our Torn Tofu Satay (page 159) and a bowl of Coconut Rice (page 112) for a super-simple meal.

Frozen broccoli is great to keep on hand to fold into soups, add to a mixed veggie stir-fry, or to toss into boiling pasta right before you drain it to add some extra greens to a meal.

Carrots

We could all use more carrots in our meals, but their ubiquity makes it easy to overlook them as a top-shelf veggie. Fix that shit now.

SAUTÉING: Cut them into rounds and sauté with some olive oil, ground coriander, and a pinch of salt until they're fork-tender. Add a tablespoon of maple syrup to take that side dish to someplace special.

ROASTING: Keep the carrots whole or cut them into sticks, toss them with olive oil and all-purpose seasoning, and roast at 400°F until they are burnt in spots, about 20 minutes. Finish with a squeeze of lemon juice and toss on some fresh herbs like dill. It makes a great, nearly painless dish.

Cauliflower

It might look like the ghost of a head of broccoli, but cauliflower is a vessel just waiting for some flavor. Give it what it wants, or it will haunt you.

ROASTING: This is simply the best way to cook cauliflower (see Sheet Pan Cauliflower with Pumpkin Seeds, page 102). Sure, you can mix up the seasoning, but this cooking method makes its flavor so much deeper and complex while removing that sulfur taste that's so synonymous with the cruciferous veggie. Roast your cauliflower florets, tossed with a little oil, at 400°F for at least 30 minutes, until tender and browned in some spots, to get the most flavor for your money.

SAUTÉING: The next best bet is sautéing cauliflower in some olive oil on the stovetop until you can get it golden in some spots. But seriously, always roast.

Steamed cauliflower is a culinary crime and should never be attempted or served.

Corn

Corn can do anything. Stop underestimating it and love it in its purest form.

SAUTÉING: Sauté corn kernels cut right off the cob with a little olive oil, salt, and pepper for a simple side.

ROASTING: Roast whole ears in the oven at 425°F for 20 minutes.

GRILLING: Brush some oil on those ears and throw them on the grill for the best side you can get with minimal effort. You can toss on coriander, chili powder, lime zest, whatever the fuck you're feeling, but grilling is by far the best way to get the most out of your corn. No grill? A grill pan is the way to go.

Greens

A side of greens doesn't need to be complicated, but you do have to find a way to love them because you're a grown-up now and you need the fiber, k?

SAUTÉING: Throw a couple handfuls in a large pan with some olive oil, a splash of soy sauce, and a minced clove of garlic and sauté until tender. You can fold this into pasta, put it on top of avocado toast, or eat as is.

BRAISING: Want to make a large pot? You gotta braise them, and we've got just the recipe (see Braised Greens, page 125).

Lighter greens like spinach do best with a simple sauté because they cook so fucking fast. Swiss chard will take a little longer, while heartier greens like kale and collards will hold up the best to braising. Whatever green you pick, know that shit will cook down to 25 percent of its original volume, so start with way more raw greens than you think you'll need. We're looking at you, spinach.

Green Beans

Green beans are perfect the less you fuck with them, particularly in the summer. Buy them when they are in season and your taste buds will thank you, no matter how you cook them.

SAUTÉING: Chop off any stems, then sauté with a little olive oil and a pinch of salt until they're tender but still have a little snap. Season with a squeeze of lemon juice at the end and a shake of garlic powder.

STEAMING: If you're gonna eat them cold as part of a salad, we like to steam them until they're bright green, about 5 minutes, then throw them in an ice bath to stop the cooking process. Drain. Then dress. It's simple as hell and perfect every time.

Summer Squash

These thin-skinned squashes are great for a quick side or filling out a pasta dish. Plus, come summer, they are cheap as hell, and if you have a friend with a garden, they start giving them away come August.

SAUTÉING: Cut them into half-moons, then sauté them with some olive oil and your favorite all-purpose seasoning. Cut them into long, thin strips and toss them with some long pasta and sauce and they'll disappear amongst the noodles. Shred them with your box grater, sauté in the same way, and watch them melt away into a creamy pile. Puree that pile, and you've got yourself a silky pasta sauce like the zucchini cream sauce in Silky Zucchini Pasta with Fresh Tomato Salsa (page 149).

GRILLING: Want to give your summer squash some deeper flavor? Cut them into planks at least a ¼ inch thick, toss them with some oil and your favorite all-purpose seasoning, and throw them on the grill. Let them cook over high heat until you get grill marks on both sides, 2 to 3 minutes each side. Serve them like that with a squeeze of citrus or cut them up into cubes and toss them into a salad like our West Coast Chopped Salad (page 71).

Winter Squash

These thick-skinned gourds start appearing in markets all over in the fall and don't leave until early spring. Whether you buy a pumpkin or an acorn squash, nearly all of them are cooked the same way, so consider this your chance to try new shit. You can cook it—just follow our lead.

ROASTING: Winter squash is made for roasting—acorn, butternut, pumpkin, kabocha, whatever squash is speaking to you. The easiest way is to crank the oven to 400°F, chop whatever hard squash you're using in half, scrape out the guts, and roast it, cut side down, until you can easily pierce the flesh with a knife, 30 to 40 minutes. Boom, roasted squash. You can also shave the skins off with a vegetable peeler, cut the squash into chunks, and toss with some olive oil, chopped onion, and all-purpose seasoning. Spread on a sheet pan and roast at 400°F until fork-tender, about 25 minutes, depending on the size of those chunks. Hell, if you grab a delicata squash, you don't even have to peel it. The skin will soften up enough to eat as it roasts.

Meal Manager

We know it's exhausting to plan for whatever the hell you and anyone else you cook for are going to eat every week. Your eyes might glaze over, and you might lose your ability to speak when confronted with the daily question "Hey, what's for dinner?" Let us take out some of that guesswork.

Here we've outlined how you can use the recipes in this book to create meals that repurpose components of the previous day's meal. This means you don't have to cook meals from scratch every single night. Cooking like this also helps cut down on grocery costs because you're repeating similar ingredients you already have on hand. Plus, leftovers don't go to waste. Want more ideas to maximize leftovers and cut down on kitchen time? Check out our Field Guides on hand pies (page 36) and enchiladas (page 169).

El Congrí de Flor

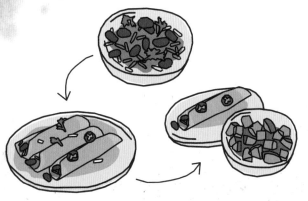

DAY 1: Make our Tomato Chickpea Fritters (page 144), 5-Minute Hummus (page 92), and Simple Side Salad with House Vinaigrette (page 50).

DAY 2: Turn your leftover fritters into sliders by serving them inside store-bought buns. Serve with Everyday Cabbage Slaw (page 67) and Tahini Cucumber Sauce (page 93).

DAY 1: Make our El Congrí de Flor (page 172).

DAY 2: Use leftover Congrí de Flor as an enchilada filling and Grilled Tomatillo and Avocado (page 108) as the sauce. Follow our recipe for Green Enchiladas (page 171) for the assembly and baking instructions.

DAY 3: Serve the rest of the enchiladas with a side of Poblano Home Fries (page 38).

DAY 1: Make Baked Butternut Squash with Tomato Lentil Sauce (page 166) with a double batch of the butternut squash.

DAY 2: Serve the leftover Baked Butternut Squash with Tomato Lentil Sauce with our Simple Side Salad with House Vinaigrette (page 50).

DAY 3: Use the extra butternut squash from day 1 to make Pumpkin Lasagna Rolls (page 180).

DAY 1: Make Green Enchiladas (page 171), and reserve the leftover Queso Blanco (page 96).

DAY 2: Eat leftover Green Enchiladas with a side of Everyday Cabbage Slaw (page 67).

DAY 3: Use the reserved Queso Blanco to make Pepper Cheese Hoagies (page 80).

DAY 1: Make Quinoa Zucchini Fritters (page 142) and serve them with our 5-Minute Hummus (page 92) and our Simple Side Salad with House Vinaigrette (page 50).

DAY 2: Serve leftover fritters on top of our Silky Zucchini Pasta (page 149) or with Cilantro Rice (page 116).

DAY 1: Make Pan-Seared Tofu Banh Mi–Inspired Sammie (page 64) with a double batch of the pan-seared tofu.

DAY 2: Serve the leftover pan-seared tofu with Sesame Noodles (page 154).

DAY 3: Eat any leftover noodles and tofu with side of Everyday Cabbage Slaw (page 67) with toasted sesame oil.

DAY 1: Make breakfast for dinner with our Savory Green Onion Toasts with a double batch of Fresh Tomato Salsa (page 26).

DAY 2: Make our Silky Zucchini Pasta (page 149) and top with the extra Fresh Tomato Salsa.

DAY 3: Serve leftover pasta with our Simple Side Salad with House Vinaigrette (page 50).

DAY 1: Make our Tomato Chickpea Fritters (page 144) and serve with our Yellow Split Pea Dip (page 118) and a salad with Dill Buttermilk Dressing (page 89).

DAY 2: Make soup from leftover Yellow Split Pea Dip and serve with a salad made with leftover Dill Buttermilk Dressing.

DAY 3: Serve leftover Tomato Chickpea Fritters over noodles dressed in our 30-Minute Marinara (page 139) and our Simple Side Salad with House Vinaigrette (page 50).

Tofu Bahn Mi

Icon Index

Acknowledgments

It's been almost ten years since our first book came out, and there's no way we would have gotten this far without the unwavering support of our readers and all the members of The Broiler Room. We literally owe y'all everything.

Thank you to our editor, Elysia Liang, whose patience and vision made this book what it is. To Kara Plikaitis, whose steady hand has shaped us since Day One. To Nick Hensley, whose artwork and talent has given life to our otherwise nonsensical ideas. To Marysarah Quinn, who always makes us feel like ours is the only book she's working on. To Diana Baroni, for her invaluable feedback and fierce spirit. Thank you to Mark McCauslin, Jessica Heim, and the rest of the team at Rodale/Penguin Random House. We appreciate all that you do.

Thank you to our agents, Kim Witherspoon and Richard Pine at Inkwell Management, for always steering us through the storms. And to Sally James, for her infectious spirit and keen eyes. We'd be lost without all of you.

MD: Thank you to my wife, Kyria, for being my sounding board, my support, and the funniest person I've ever met. My recipes have never been better and that's all because of you. Without your ideas, feedback, and insatiable appetite, this book wouldn't exist. Thank you for loving me. Thank you to Roxy for being the best, and Jade for her measured insanity. To Sanders for the fat rain and hospitality. And lastly, thanks to my family for making sure I always stay on the right side of crazy.

MH: Thank you to my dad, Byron, for his support and allowing me to publicly share his undying devotion to eggplants. Thank you to Kat McPhee, Jac Vanek, and Jared Monaco for being good taste testers and even better friends. Thanks to Brian Cullen for roasting me more than anything in this cookbook. Thank you to my fiancée, Alexis Linkletter, for her unconditional love and support throughout the production of this book. She's been a pillar of strength and a well of inspiration and relentless encouragement, not just to this book but to our company. I would be lost without y'all.

General Index

COOKING OR CLEANING.
NOBODY EATS FOR FREE.

END